Wearable Art

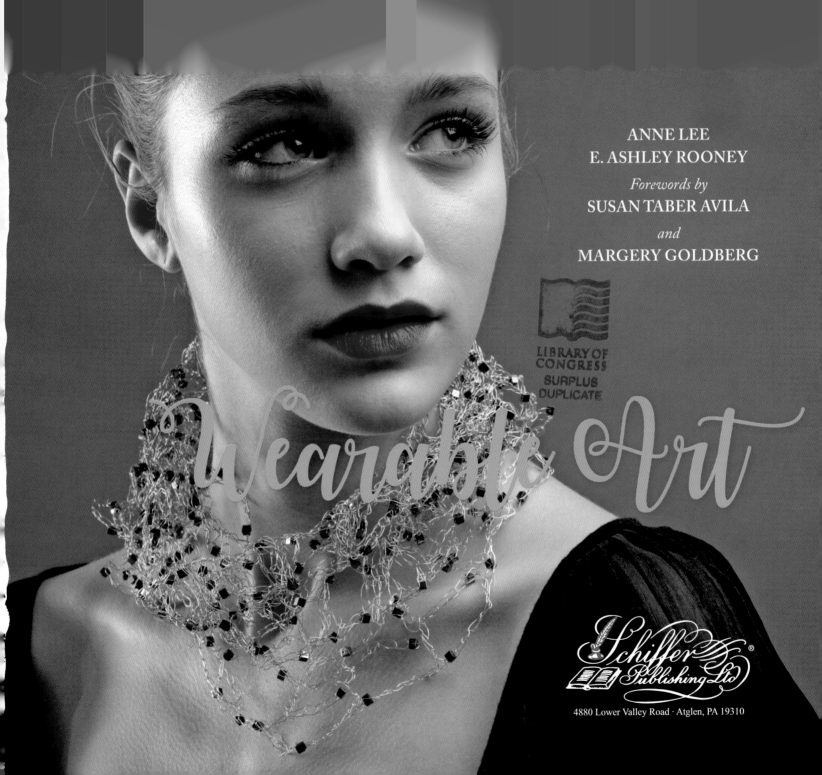

ANNE LEE
E. ASHLEY ROONEY

Forewords by
SUSAN TABER AVILA

and

MARGERY GOLDBERG

Wearable Art

Schiffer
Publishing Ltd
4880 Lower Valley Road · Atglen, PA 19310

Artistry in Fiber, Vol. 1: Wall Art, Anne Lee and E. Ashley Rooney, Foreword by Marcia Young, Introduction by Meredith Re' Grimsley, ISBN 978-0-7643-5304-8

Artistry in Fiber, Vol. 2: Sculpture, Anne Lee and E. Ashley Rooney, Foreword by Lois Russell, Introduction by Adrienne Sloane, ISBN 978-0-7643-5342-0

Encaustic Art in the Twenty-First Century, Anne Lee and E. Ashley Rooney, Foreword by Kim Bernard, Afterword by Ellen Koment, ISBN 978-0-7643-5023-8

Other Schiffer Books on Related Subjects:

Making Good: An Inspirational Guide to Being an Artist Craftsman, Jacklyn Scott, Kristin Müller, and Tommy Simpson, Foreword by Stuart Kestenbaum, ISBN 978-0-7643-5287-4

Fashion Print Design: From the Idea to the Final Fabric, Angel Fernández and Daniela Santos Quartino, ISBN 978-0-7643-4591-3

Art Jewelry Today: Europe, Catherine Mallette, ISBN 978-0-7643-4678-1

Designed by Brenda McCallum
Cover design by Brenda McCallum
Type set in NewsGothic/Adobe Caslon

Front cover image: Jenne Gilles *(Vincent Gotti).* Back cover images, clockwise from left: Daiga Henson and Sarmite Svilis *(Marc Hall Photography).* Jera Rose Petal Lodge *(Nash Quinn).* Ariane Mariane. Front endsheet: Claire Prebble *(Alessandro Saponi).* Title page: Zuzana Graus Rudavská *(Oto Skalicky).* Page 3: Amy Nguyen. Page 4: Maja Houtman. Page 7: Rebecca Wendlandt *(Todd and Barbara Photography).* Page 8: *Left* Eva Camacho-Sánchez *(Maureen Sullivan). Right* Lisa Klakulak *(Mary Vogel).* Page 9: Daiga Henson and Sarmite Svilis *(Peter Groesbeck).* Page 10: Ana Lisa Hedstrom *(Barry Shapiro).* Page 11: Lauri Chambers. Page 98: David K. Chatt *(Dana Moore).* Page 99: David K. Chatt *(Kathryn Gremley).* Page 100: *Left* Yong Joo Kim. *Right* Kathryn Scimone Stanko *(Tiffany Whitfield).* Page 101: Tina Lazzarine. Back endsheet: Jera Rose Petal Lodge.

ISBN: 978-0-7643-5399-4

Printed in China

Published by Schiffer Publishing, Ltd.
4880 Lower Valley Road | Atglen, PA 19310
Phone: (610) 593-1777; Fax: (610) 593-2002
E-mail: Info@schifferbooks.com | Web: www.schifferbooks.com

For our complete selection of fine books on this and related subjects, please visit our website at www.schifferbooks.com. You may also write for a free catalog.

Schiffer Publishing's titles are available at special discounts for bulk purchases for sales promotions or premiums. Special editions, including personalized covers, corporate imprints, and excerpts, can be created in large quantities for special needs. For more information, contact the publisher.

We are always looking for people to write books on new and related subjects. If you have an idea for a book, please contact us at proposals@schifferbooks.com.

CONTENTS

PREFACE

When we decided to compile a book on contemporary fiber art, we quickly realized what an enormous and potentially daunting project we had taken on. One book could not begin to adequately showcase the amazing creative energy of fiber artists and the fascinating directions they are pushing the medium. With three books planned—Wall Art, Sculpture, and Wearable Art—our year-long journey began.

Wearable Art explores the space where fashion and art meet, an interactive space in which the wearer both influences and is influenced by the art itself. The body breathes life, shape, and movement into a piece, which in turn alters perception, mood, or feeling. Through wearable art—be it a felted brooch or a dress made of book pages—the wearer can find personal expression unavailable in a world of mass production.

We asked our two foreword writers, Susan Taber Avila and Margery Goldberg, to explore the past and present trends in the ever-evolving world of art to wear, and we thank them for rising to the challenge.

Join us and discover an endlessly fascinating and evolving medium that has always been part of our history and will be part of our future.

INTRODUCTION

For centuries, artists have explored, explained, and enhanced our world. While that concept has not altered, today's artists are more apt to break with tradition, reject classic notions of beauty, and express their inner world. Old definitions of art have become obsolete. Traditional methods, processes, and materials are evolving in fascinating and sometimes perplexing directions. Contemporary art is fluid, dynamic, challenging, and open to multiple interpretations.

The resurgence of fiber art beautifully illustrates these trends. Through much of its history, fiber came exclusively from plants and animals and was crafted—mostly by women—to serve domestic and utilitarian functions. The feminist movement appropriated fiber art in the 1970s, recognizing its versatility as well as its ability to yield a vast range of expression.

Artists today expand their use of natural materials, such as cowhide and plant stalks, and explore unexpected synthetics—strands of acrylic paint, artificial hair, plastic, fiberglass, tape, and wire. They combine different fiber techniques together in a single piece, braiding, tacking, weaving, and knitting in seemingly endless variations. They push technical processes, whether by knitting with glass or by felting with silk. They cross-pollinate mediums, incorporating photographs, paint, metal, and all manner of found or repurposed objects. They explore social, political, economic, and environmental issues, as well as tell their own personal stories. They turn inward, they look back, they look to the future.

The language of textiles is rich in metaphors, many of which allude to connection and conversation. Just by picking up a strand, whether it is a gorgeous strand of cotton fiber or a shiny strand of copper wire, fiber artists begin to use the physical mark of a stitch to tell their story. For us, the artists of today not only tell the stories of today but also create exciting energy for tomorrow. Like today's authors, they are delineating our stories for future generations. They differ from state to state, country to country. To find them, we talked to gallery owners, museum curators, and the artists themselves; read fiber magazines and books; researched textile societies and organizations; read biographies, searched awards, perused exhibitions. We explored the work of literally hundreds of artists.

Our intention in undertaking a three-volume series exploring contemporary fiber art was to take a fresh look at the magical and insightful ways in which today's fiber artists have interpreted life in this century. We wanted those who would bring strength, excitement, passion, and variety to this series. We believe we have found them.

ARTISTRY IN FIBER:

Art to Wear

FOREWORD

Understanding Wearable Art *Susan Taber Avila*

A new survey of wearable art is long overdue. Many artists who create wearable compositions at the intersection where fashion meets art deserve to be recognized. In *Artistry in Fiber, Vol. 3: Wearable Art,* Anne Lee and E. Ashley Rooney contribute to the ongoing dialogue, presenting a selection of artists whose work explores the malleability and lusciousness of textiles in relation to the body.

The term wearable art is often used to describe garments that bridge art, design, craft, and fashion. This broad category encourages much debate when classifying relevance or stature within the greater arena of fine art. Included in this field are conceptual works that either conform to or allude to the body, as well as beautifully crafted unique garments that convey personal expression in an aesthetic manner. Fashion is a popular subject for many artists due to its obvious connection to identity and culture, yet wearable art is often at arm's length from fashion. Fashion embraces the *zeitgeist*—it identifies with a specific moment in time—while wearable art is essentially anti-fashion in that it is independent of current style trends and aims for a classic, innovative exemption from mainstream fashion.

Commonalities between fashion and wearable art include the objective of personal adornment. Although there are many reasons to wear clothes, evidence of tattooing on ancient mummies supports a plausible argument that decoration was the most compelling motivator for humans to adopt clothing. Historical examples of aesthetic details on dress include jeweled embellishments on Byzantine robes, ornamental Renaissance slashing that reveals colorful linings,

sixteenth-century elaborate blackwork embroidery, and protrusions of lace from head (the ruff) to toe (shoe roses) in the early seventeenth century. In the eighteenth century, a myriad of three-dimensional embellishments appear in combination with fine silk brocades, while the nineteenth century emphasizes a variety of body structures exaggerated by crinolines, sleeve puffs, bustles, and tight corsets.

While there are anti-fashion movements throughout history, the extreme body subjugation of the nineteenth century created an opportunity for artists to show an interest in reform clothing, and the artistic dress movement offered an alternative, albeit ridiculed, mode of dressing for a few daring individuals.

In the early twentieth century, the showmanship of Paul Poiret paved the way for a more general acceptance of new body shapes, ironically ones that referenced historical garments such as the neoclassical empire waist or the Japanese-influenced kimono form. He claims to have been inspired by everything including historical costume, ethnographic textiles, and many contemporary art forms. At this time, many artists felt free to work in the arena of design, and designers often looked to artists for inspiration. Elsa Schiaparelli's garment silhouettes were rather conventional, but the imagery on her clothing clearly demonstrates her connection with Dada and surrealist art movements. Another significant influence of the time was the bold and colorful costumes from the Ballets Russes. And, the painter Sonia Delaunay made both paintings and clothing in her inimitable simple geometric style; her original textiles, while clearly derived from her artwork, were designed for production rather than one-of-a-kind creations.

The appearance of expressive, unique, handcrafted garments coincided with the hippie movement of the 1960s. Hippies cultivated an anti-fashion look that also encompassed a feeling of nostalgia. There was a renewed interest in the handcrafts of grandmothers as well as a desire to imitate the beautiful ethnographic textiles becoming more and more visible in western culture. When Yoshiko Wada introduced Japanese shibori dyeing techniques in a 1974 Berkeley Fiberworks workshop, she instigated a surface design revolution. Her subsequent books on shibori techniques and development of the World Shibori Network helped make this magical resist process a ubiquitous method integral to any hand-dyeing education. Ana Lisa Hedstrom

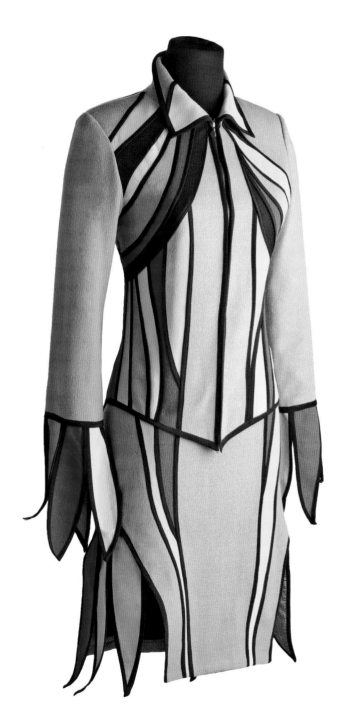

was one of Wada's first students, and from that basic instruction Hedstrom continued on a path of self-discovery to become one of the leading innovators of shibori dyeing techniques. Hedstrom continues to push the envelope, working with both natural and synthetic dyes as well as thermoplastic materials. While Hedstrom's own work moves between art for the wall and art for the body, her influence can be seen on several of the artists in this book, such as the well-balanced compositions of Amy Nguyen's outerwear.

Many artists in the 1970s began using the body as a canvas for their paintings and sculptures, experimenting with wearable forms and often adopting traditional craft techniques such as weaving, knitting, crocheting, and hand dyeing. Textile processes were at the forefront of this movement, and artists worked on the simultaneous development of surface and structure. This led to an art-to-wear movement that by the 1980s had formed into a cohesive field of study with pivotal exhibitions and significant publications showcasing the work of wearable garments by artists. The functional quality of these art pieces allowed for a commercial marketplace that sold one-of-a-kind and limited production garments. The pinnacle of success for many artists was selling their work at Julie: Artisans' Gallery in New York City or Obiko in San Francisco. Both have since closed; however, there is a relatively new digital Obiko archive on the Fine Arts Museum of San Francisco Textile Arts Council website.

The late twentieth century saw a proliferation of fashion designers incorporating ideas borrowed from earlier artisans and often (re)discovering textiles and surface design. As a result, fashion itself became more interesting, and new body structures and shapes emerged. For example, the new wave of Japanese designers including Issey Miyake and Rei Kawakubo and conceptual thinkers like Martin Margiela and Hussein Chalayan pushed form into new directions, while John Galliano, Alexander McQueen, and Jean-Paul Gaultier played with surface texture and embellishment. In many ways, anti-fashion became fashionable. Big blockbuster exhibitions of well-known fashion designers emerged as if to validate the designer as artist.

As the twenty-first century began, many of the early leaders in art-to-wear focused their attention more towards making art for the wall and/or discreet objects with less emphasis on the

Wearable art may be confused with costume design; costume usually describes clothing designed for performance or theatre when its goal is to assist the narrative. When the garments themselves form the narrative, then wearable art is a better description. Sharon Kallis develops a narrative with her conceptual textiles sourced from local plant materials. The concept behind her linen shirt speaks eloquently about labor and craft. The extremely slow process of growing a linen shirt from seed, spinning flax plants into yarn, and knitting them together confronts the idea of time and place belying the garment's austere appearance.

In contrast to the esoteric nature of Kallis's garments, but with the same degree of obsessive detail, are the intricate and fanciful creations by Claire Prebble. Her beautiful filigree lacework of wire, beads, embroidery, plaiting, and stitching allude to mythical, mystical, and romantic escapades. Rebecca Wendlandt's garments are also meticulous and immaculately executed; her exuberant designs tell a story through manipulated fabric and innovative silhouettes, which are thoughtfully engineered and constructed.

A different type of engineering comes from the formation of felt, and many of the artists presented in this book work in this medium. Felting is one of the oldest textile techniques in existence where heat, moisture, and agitation bond wool fibers (roving) together to form a fabric. The wool can also be bound to other pre-existing textiles, resulting in sheer, texturized, lightweight fabrics. Polly Stirling and Sachiko Kotaka popularized this laminated technique, called nuno felting, in the 1990s.

The very nature of felted constructions lends itself to whimsical forms and soft structures, as seen in the wonderful hats by Lauri Chambers and Jean Hicks, or the quirky bags by Lisa Klakulak and Ariane Mariane. Jenne Giles takes advantage of the structural aspect of felt in her multi-layered accessories while Eva Camacho-Sánchez's Barcelona vests are sumptuous, painterly forms.

The authors tell me that the works in this book were chosen for "wearability" and accessibility. Obviously, this can only be a small sample of wearable art as selected through their discriminating taste. A common thread throughout is the mark of the hand and the sumptuousness of cloth. Handmade, hand dyed, and embellished textiles permeate the selections, which showcase personal adornment through their unique expression on the body.

body. A new group, spurred by do-it-yourself thinking, became part of a burgeoning maker culture, and artists were once again newly discovering textile techniques. Almost any textile technique can now be learned through a YouTube video, and websites like Etsy provide accessible ways to sell individual creations. As the boundaries between art, craft, design, and fashion merge, it is difficult to define wearable art in the present day, and ambivalence towards an isolated definition is probably a healthy stance to take. The international Surface Design Association does an excellent job of presenting the best of wearable pieces through its highly acclaimed journal, while organizations such as New Zealand's World of Wearable Art (WOW) have elevated the quality of wearable one-of-a-kind creations through their rigorous jury process.

Courtesy of Lee Weisz.

Susan Taber Avila
Emeryville, California

I create textile artwork to enhance our perception of contemporary culture. Although I am best known for my wall hangings and sculptures, my wearable constructions intersect art, design, and fashion. I design by imagining the body as an armature for my garments, rather than as a shape to conform to. My work promotes sustainability through the reclamation of pre-consumer and post-consumer waste, and I explore new methods and materials to develop new textile structures and to interlock meaning within the structure. Through the utilization of a water-soluble substrate, polyvinyl alcohol (PVA), I piece together remnants from the fashion and interior design industries. In this way, I create objects of beauty from textiles that might otherwise end up in a landfill.

The pieces *Splash* and *Falling Leaves* are part of a series inspired by nature, especially the organization and perception of nature by humans. The red garments shown here, all made from textile waste, are part of a larger collection focusing on women and their health, inspired by the red dress symbol used by the National Institutes of Health and the American Heart Association to promote awareness of cardiovascular disease, the number one killer of women.

Falling Leaves. Recycled fabric scraps sewn to cotton twill understructure, floating elements developed with stitching and dissolving polyvinyl alcohol. 2011. Model: Haley Gilhooley.

All art images courtesy of John Bagley.

12

Splash. Machine stitched and dissolved polyvinyl alcohol, stiffened net modules sewn to polyester fabric understructure. 2011. Model: Andrea Castillo Avila.

You've Come a Long Way Baby. Recycled sample fabrics sewn to undergarment of recycled fabric. 2015. Model: Leticia Garay.

Vascular Expression. Pre-consumer textile waste cut into strips and sewn to a recycled fabric underdress. 2014. Model: Leticia Garay.

15

Laura G. Berman
Philomath, Oregon

Memories of joyously dancing with scarves and recruiting adults to teach me to sew and knit mark my lifelong passion for clothing and textiles. When I reflect on my early fascination with this art form and my grandfather who came to the United States as a tailor, I know it is bound into my DNA.

Wool fiber is very "alive." The hairs embrace each other and will grasp onto other fabrics and materials. It demands total attentiveness when attempting to master its willful and challenging quirks. Using wool as my medium enables me to create unexpected textures and to build three-dimensional structures for my wearable art and sculptures. I prefer completing as much of my work as possible during the wet-felting process without the need to do any sewing.

Nature's infinite beauty and imagination are often my inspirational source for ideas. What could be closer to nature than working with my hands, using water, olive oil soap, and fibers from an animal?

My work is textural, colorful, whimsical, and animated. I love including an element of surprise, dimensional embellishments, and, if possible, a pinch of wry humor. As a quietly spiritual person, I'm pleased with my creation when my work "sings" with energy.

Paisley Handbag. Merino, Corriedale wool, and novelty yarns; wet felting with resists. 9.75" × 11" × 3". 2015.

Spectral Colors Handbag. Bluefaced Leicester wool, handspun and novelty yarn, and wool nepps; wet felted. 15" × 17" × 7". 2015.

Circles and Leaves Pocket Scarf. Merino wool, silk chiffon, novelty yarns, and wet-felted beads; wet felting onto fabric base (front and back sides are identical). 36" × 11.5". 2012.

Paisley Pocket Scarf. Merino wool, silk gauze, novelty yarns, oil paintstick, and wet-felted beads; wet felting onto fabric base (front and back sides are identical). 35.5" × 11.5". 2012.

All images courtesy of David Paul Bales.

Photo by Joyce Eichacker.

Eva Camacho-Sánchez
Florence, Massachusetts

I learned to create from my mother, who grew up in a poor, rural village in the 1940s, and had no choice but to make her own clothes, sheets, and other textiles. Her passion for creating and the importance of self-sufficiency were instilled in me at an early age, although my artistic passion only came alive when I discovered the amazing qualities of wool and the wonderful art of felting as an adult.

Traditionally, felt is created by using water, soap, wool, and agitation. Felting takes time, physical labor, and patience. Most of my items are made with wool from local farms, using Icelandic and Romney varieties for housewares and merino for wearables. I buy the fleeces directly from farmers, then wash, dye, and card them myself.

Barcelona Vest #4. Nuno felted and hand dyed, 100 percent merino wool, 100 percent silk fabric. 2015. Photographer: Maureen Sullivan.

I usually start by hand dyeing the wool with natural dyes I have created myself from plant matter. I then felt it together with fine silk to create lightweight nuno felt. To create patterns on the silk, I use techniques such as free-motion embroidery, hand stitching, beading, and printing. My work is the result of the fusion of the ancient art form of feltmaking with modern techniques to create new and elegant styles.

Barcelona Vest #1. Nuno felted and hand dyed, 100 percent merino wool, 100 percent silk fabric. 2015. Photographer: Maureen Sullivan.

Koko Vest #2. Nuno felted and hand dyed, 100 percent merino wool, 100 percent silk fabric. 2016.

OPPOSITE
LEFT *Lace Vest #4.* Nuno felted, fifty percent merino wool, fifty percent silk fabric. 2016.

RIGHT *Barcelona Vest #11.* Nuno felted and hand dyed, 100 percent merino wool, 100 percent silk fabric. 2016.

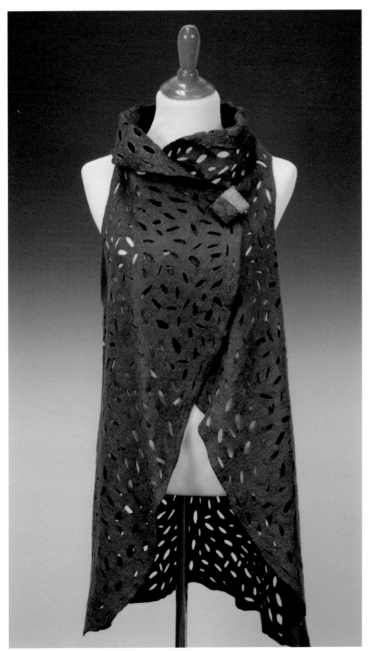

Lauri Chambers
Nordland, Washington

"I wish I could give people cause to be as ecstatic as I was
the day the wild bird rode atop my head."

I have always liked making stuff. I like marginal technologies, color relationships, and simple, satisfying forms. I want to make hats that, although they may draw attention to themselves, do not overshadow the people who wear them. I want each hat to suit its particular wearer aesthetically and psychologically and bring some kind of pleasure into the life of the person who wears it.

Working with the materials is always magical. I am still surprised that wool fiber, warm water, and soap can become such a strong, warm, beautiful fabric.

I like surprises.

Swoop. Hand felted merino wool. 7" × 8.25" × 8.25". 2015.

OPPOSITE
Twisted. Hand felted merino wool. 6" × 8.25" × 8.25". 2015.

Drift. Hand felted merino wool. 7" × 8" × 8". 2015.

out THERE. Hand felted merino wool. 12" × 8" × 8". 2015.

Flair. Hand felted merino wool. 7.25" × 10" × 10". 2015.

Susan Kathleen Doyle
San Geronimo, California

I have always had a drive to experiment and make unique things with my hands. Materials inspire me—scraps of beautiful silk, zippers from a recycling store. I enjoy taking these materials and using them to explore particular ideas or compositions from a variety of perspectives. My art is inspired by color and relationships, both personal, political, and in nature. For example, when one of my friends in my art group was diagnosed with a recurrence of cancer, we set to work making art hats for her to wear as she lost her hair. We laughed and cried together and were amazed at her strength and humor. When she asked us to make a cover for her coffin, we met and stitched together pieces of beautiful silk she gave us. This *Cycle of Life* dress was begun with remnants of the silk from her "celebration banner," which is what she called the cover. The dress is a reminder of the beautiful process that is life—from the new green leaves and buds, to blossoming, to wilting, and finally returning to the earth to begin the cycle again.

I use techniques traditionally used in fiber art in non-traditional ways—weaving zippers or pages from a book, making a dress that has more meaning than just a fashion statement. I like to think about who would wear these. Could it be you?

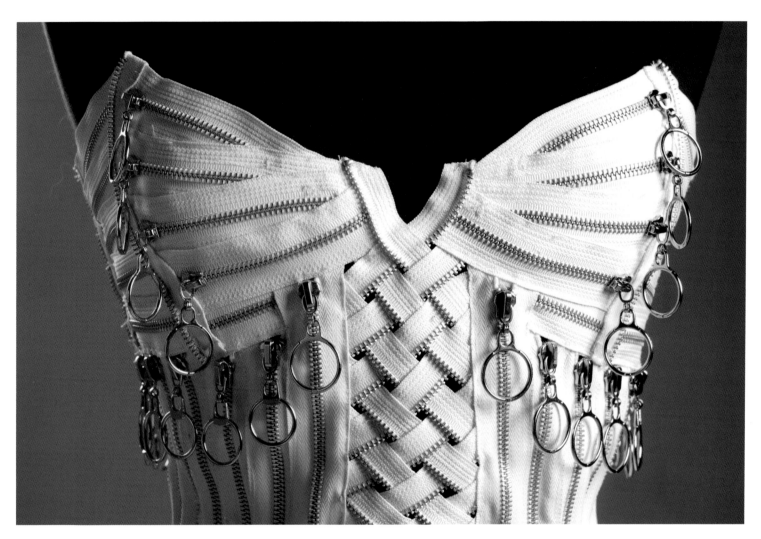

OPPOSITE AND DETAIL
Marilyn. Zippers and thread. 21" × 12" × 9". 2015.
Courtesy of Dana Davis.

Julia. Zippers, fabric, and thread. 29" × 28" × 9". 2015.
Courtesy of Dana Davis.

Scarlet. Zippers, thread, and organza.
32" × 11" × 9". 2015.
Courtesy of Dana Davis.

Cycle of Life. Silk, organza, and thread.
70" × 36". 2013. Courtesy of Jay Daniels,
Black Cat Studio.

Carmen. Fabric, zippers, paper maps, and thread.
65" × 20" × 30". 2016. Courtesy of Dana Davis.

Jenne Giles
Joshua Tree, California

I began working with wool in 2005 when I started my own business in San Francisco with the goal of making wearable art. Feltmaking was completely new to me, and I poured many hours into teaching myself this new craft that combined many things that I dearly loved: sculptural form, painterly color, and useful design that could be worn out in the world. This new adventure led me in many fascinating directions. Over time, I have exhibited these felted pieces at nationally renowned events and international exhibitions.

By 2009, I had ventured back into the world of fine art, exploring the possibilities of felted wool as a painterly medium. A year later, I was invited to write a book titled *Felt Fashion: Couture Projects from Garments to Accessories* detailing some of the similarities I found between making felt and traditional garment-making techniques. In 2012, I branched from wearable art into sculptural work and installation; in 2015, I was honored to be the Kimball Gallery Artist-in-Residence at the deYoung Museum in San Francisco.

Every day I learn new things as I continue on this wonderful journey exploring wool's artistic potential as painting, sculpture, and exciting wearable work.

Rose Dress. Merino wool and tussah silk (nuno felt). 2010. Photography by Moja Ma'at.

Rose Scarf. Merino wool and tussah silk (nuno felt). 8" × 60". 2010 (original design dates to 2006). Photography by Moja Ma'at.

Lichen Collar. Merino wool
and bombyx silk (nuno felt).
25" × 20". 2014.
Photography by Vincent Gotti.

Wings. Merino wool and bombyx silk (nuno felt). 25" × 60". 2014. Photography by Vincent Gotti.

Tendril Wrap. Merino and angora wool, tussah silk (nuno felt, shibori dyed). 45" × 65". 2010. Photography by Moja Ma'at.

I have been creating shibori fabrics for over thirty-five years and I continue to find ideas to explore. For several decades, I worked primarily in silk, creating one-of-a-kind pieced coats. Then I began to explore the possibilities of polyester, which can be permanently pleated—a perfect material for sculptural garments. At this time, I had returned "to the wall," creating studio art quilts and interior art. I found there was always a "discussion" between creating wearables or artwork. One use inspired the other.

Our Great Blue and Black Sea was created for the wall, but I immediately saw that the concept would also work for a costume. *Amphitrite, Queen of the Sea*, was included in World of Wearable Art – International Design Competition (WOW) in New Zealand. It refers to our vast oceans beleaguered by oil spills. Amphitrite cries tears of brown oil. I continued this series with both synthetic felt and polyester organza.

I like designing, so I have never completely stopped producing clothing. Now I want to make simple jackets and accessories that anyone can wear at any time of day. At the same time, I have rekindled my interest in natural dyes, especially working directly on fine cottons and linens with thickened natural indigo. Who knows what will motivate me next?

Ana Lisa Hedstrom
La Honda, California

Morning Glory Dress and Coat. Hand stitched and manipulated polyester, transfer print, and heat set. 2007. Photo: Barry Shapiro.

Winter Vest. Synthetic felt, stitched, and heat set; dye sublimation transfer print. 2007. Photo: Barry Shapiro.

Amphitrite, Queen of the Sea. Synthetic felt made from recycled plastic bottles, dye sublimation, transfer print. 2012. Photo: Kim Harrington.

37

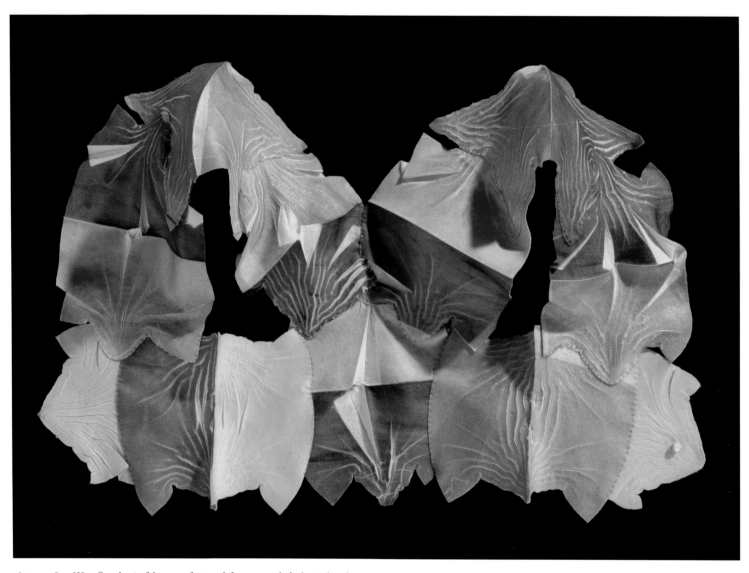

Autumn Leaf Vest. Synthetic felt manufactured from recycled plastic bottles;
hand stitched, heat set, and transfer printed. 2012. Photo: Don Tuttle.

Felt Jacket. Synthetic felt trim. *Scarf*. Heat set, dye sublimation transfer print. 2007. Photo: Barry Shapiro.

Digital Print Coat. Digital print based on arashi shibori swatch, dye sublimation on polyester. 2005. Photo: Barry Shapiro.

Daiga Henson and Sarmite Svilis
East Windsor, New Jersey

We are two sisters born and raised in Latvia, a small country by the Baltic Sea. We have been working in collaboration, making one-of-a-kind coats and jackets, for over twenty-five years. We apply our knowledge of sewing, patternmaking, and tailoring to craft timeless pieces of wearable art. Our Latvian roots inspire our designs as we draw inspiration from national costumes and the traditional festive outfits of peasants, craftsmen, fishermen, and other ordinary people.

Using a variety of natural fabrics such as wool, cashmere, silk, and linen, we employ a collage technique of piecing together a variety of patterns, colors, and textures into our wearable art. Individual segments of each garment are technically and visually held together by black silk to embrace the human form, while accentuating the elegant movements of the wearer.

We believe that, regardless of fashion, trends, and time, the aesthetics of the female figure should be presented in the most beautiful light.

Baltic Swing Coat. Wool, cashmere, linen, and silk crêpe de Chine; piecework, silk piping, and draping. 2016. Courtesy Marc Hall Photography.

Ulster Coat. Cashmere wool and
handwoven chenille; collage, piecework,
silk piping, and embroidery. 2006.

Foliage Mantelet Suit. Wool gabardine and silk crêpe de Chine; draping, piecework, silk piping, and embroidery. 2006.

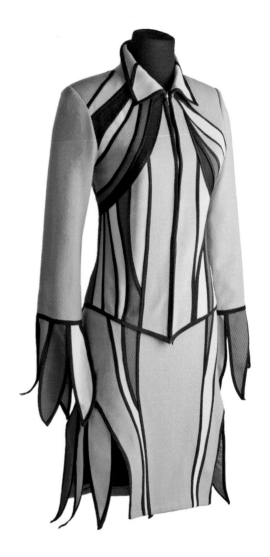

Tulip Suit. Wool crêpe, wool gabardine, and silk crêpe de Chine; collage and silk piping. 2013. Photography by Peter Groesbeck.

Kurland Coat. Wool crêpe, cashmere, wool gabardine, silk crêpe de Chine; collage and silk piping. 2016. Courtesy Marc Hall Photography.

Golden Redingote Suit. Cashmere wool and silk crêpe de Chine; piecework, inlay silk piping, and embroidery. 2006.

Artist in *Component Venting Hat*. Hand felted finn/merino with detachable headband, hand blocked, and finished. 2011.

Jean Hicks
Seattle, Washington

As a milliner and feltmaker, my work is about the transformation of body lines. I create architectural sculptures using a mix of wool and thread, notions, and both colorations and natural dyes. I was born in California and raised in the Pacific Northwest, close to mountains and ocean; my work is inspired by both the practical and fantastical found in the natural abundance of these regions.

I have designed and fabricated for Teatro ZinZanni, Maureen Whiting Dance Company, and New City Theater productions, and worked as an assistant to performance/fiber artists Nick Cave and Joan Livingstone. I have exhibited my hats in the Ukraine, Finland, Italy, Scotland, and the Netherlands; and nationally at the prestigious Smithsonian Craft Show and Philadelphia Museum of Art Craft Show. I have also shown hundreds of children in the Northwest how to create headwear and taught adults at the school of the Art Institute of Chicago, Haystack School of Craft, Penland School of Crafts, Antioch University, and Pratt Fine Arts Center in Seattle.

Altai Ice Princess. Hand felted merino/alpaca, repurposed mink, hand blocked, and finished. 2013.

All images courtesy of Jan Cook Photography.

▲ *Squid.* Hand felted merino, hand blocked, and finished. 2010.

◀ *Syrah.* Hand felted and blocked merino/alpaca, hand dyed, and stitched. 2011.

▶ *Tangelo.* Hand felted finn wool, stitched, and blocked. 2010.

Sharon Kallis
*Vancouver, British Columbia,
Canada*

Through my "one mile diet" approach to sourcing art supplies, I discover the material potential in local landscapes. Preferring company to working alone, I invite others along for the journey, and we learn much faster figuring things out together—connecting traditional hand techniques with invasive plant species and garden waste or "unventing" almost-lost agricultural traditions. I consider myself unbelievably fortunate that I get to do what I do for a living and have people around me that support my zany ideas by participating in a million ways. I am the author of *Common Threads: Weaving Community through Collaborative Eco-Art*, a field guide for anyone wishing to explore unwanted plants for creative purposes.

The images here include a top I designed and knit using linen I originally held in my hand as seed. Instead of depending on others far away to clothe me, my peers and neighbors helped me source seeds, prep land, plant, weed, harvest, build processing equipment, perfect linen spinning, and harvest local dye plants. It took three years from seeding the first crop to having enough fiber of a decent quality worthy of knitting! I wear my community with me in this fiber top. Other images are from an installation of shoes made as a method of investigating plants while in residence in Cataluña, Spain. Four directions for harvest resulted in four pairs of shoes. People were invited to walk fifty steps in my shoes before the shoes were left as a biodegradable directional compass.

▲ Artist in *soil.seed.shirt*. Knit top made with local linen dyed with local plants. 2013–2015. Photo: David Gowman.

► Process. Community harvesting flax for linen used in artist's shirt. 2014.

▲ Fresh flax stalks, linen stricks, spun and knit linen samples. 2014.

◀ *Northern Shoes*: "Walking selfie" woven shoes made with grasses and pine needles. 2015.

▶ *50 feet in my shoes* durational performance in which anyone who fit the woven shoes was invited to walk in the direction from which the shoe fibers were harvested; western shoes in foreground. 2015.

Lisa Klakulak
Asheville, North Carolina

In my undergraduate studies in fiber arts, form was of little consideration in comparison to surface design, and, as I was soon to realize, form was the missing element. Animal fiber has a well-known though unique ability to mat, but understanding that this unspun fiber could be matted into a fabric simultaneously to taking on dimensional form amounted to a life-changing event. I entered into a three-year residency focusing solely on the shrinkage of fiber as an artistic process, exploring both sculpting as well as surface design and inevitably establishing my business, Strongfelt.

Wool is associated with insulating, protective qualities, and form allows for containment, which equates security. Handbags hold items that represent our fleeting notion of comfort and control: they hold our ability to go anywhere, to access our shelter, to connect with people we know; they hold drugs to block pain, whether physical or emotional; and, of course, our purchasing power to obtain whatever it is we need to soothe us on this strange human journey. Handbags and their contents fortify us against the hard realities of the world.

I implement surface patterns that represent basic materials humans have used to build walls of containment: stone, brick, fencing, and woodgrain. I use free-motion machine stitching to tighten up designs as well as to stiffen the felt and stylize the bag forms, evoking objects of necessity such as canteens, baskets, boats, and hammocks.

Hammock. Icelandic wool, alpaca and silk fibers, cotton and waxed linen thread, plastic tubing, magnets; partial felt surface patterned, free-motion machine embroidered, hand stitched. 14" × 20.5" × 6". 2013. Photo: Mary Vogel.

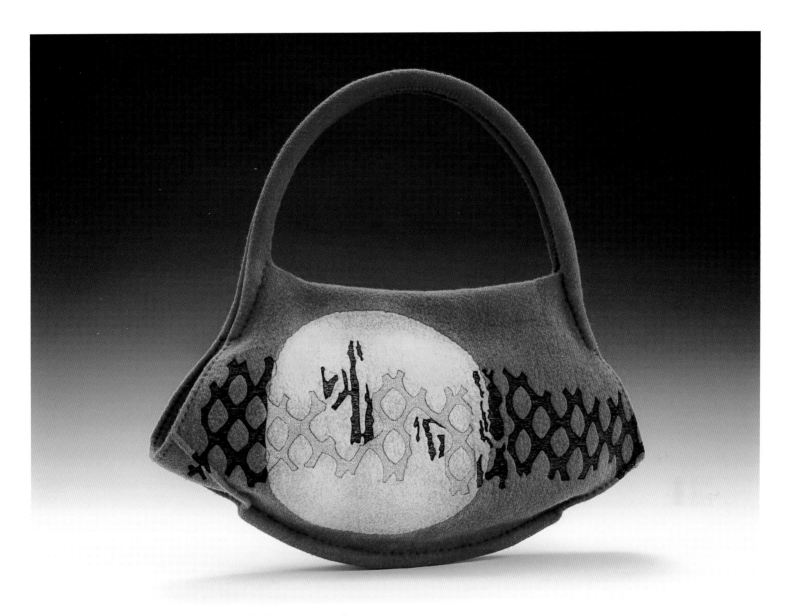

Obscured Light. Merino wool fiber, cotton thread, plastic tubing, and magnets; naturally dyed with cutch, madder, and cochineal extracts; free-motion machine embroidered, hand stitched, and shellac stiffened. 19" × 18" × 5". 2014. Photo: Stewart Stokes.

Deep Pockets. Icelandic, alpaca, and merino wool fiber, silk fiber, cotton and waxed linen thread, plastic tubing, magnets, shellac; naturally dyed with cochineal and osage natural dyes; wet felted hollow form, partial felt surface patterned, free-motion machine embroidered, hand stitched. 13" × 17" × 5". 2014. Photo: Steve Mann.

◄ *Tracks.* Icelandic, alpaca, and merino wool fiber, silk fiber, cotton and waxed linen thread, plastic tubing, magnets, shellac; naturally dyed with cochineal and osage natural dyes; wet felted hollow form, partial felt surface patterned, free-motion machine embroidered, hand stitched. 13" × 13" × 4". 2014. Photo: Steve Mann.

▼ *Canteen Handbag.* Wool, cotton, and waxed linen thread, plastic tubing, magnets; wet felted, partial felt surface patterned, naturally dyed, free-motion machine embroidered, hand stitched. Approximately 13" × 14" × 3.5" each. 2015. Photo: Steve Mann.

Ariane Mariane
Paris, France

I am a German artist who has lived and worked in Paris for over twenty years. Motivated by the belief that art should be part of our everyday life and not be limited to museums and art galleries, I create luxury wearable art and accessories as well as visual arts like wall hangings and sculptures. Trained in architecture and graphical textile design, I combine graphic design and fiber art to make pieces in a fancy and playful style. Each item is created by hand, in a time-consuming fiber painting and felting process and often adorned by free-motion stitching and/or hand painting.

With my one-of-a-kind art to wear, I want people to stand out of the crowd and add a touch of sparkle to everyday life.

Rusty Flower (hat) and *Golden Square* (tunic). Nuno felted, merino wool fibers and silk fabric; free-motion embroidery, hand painting. 40" × 34". 2015.

◄ *Seed*. Merino wool fibers, linen fabric; wet felting, free-motion embroidery. 16.5" × 9.5". 2015.

► *Silverflower*. Merino wool fibers, linen fabric, silver thread; wet felting, free-motion embroidery. 16.5" × 9.5". 2015.

Red NYC. Nuno felted merino wool and silk, natural dyes, embroidered in free-motion stitching, application of recycled or hand-painted silk fabrics. 35" × 21". 2015.

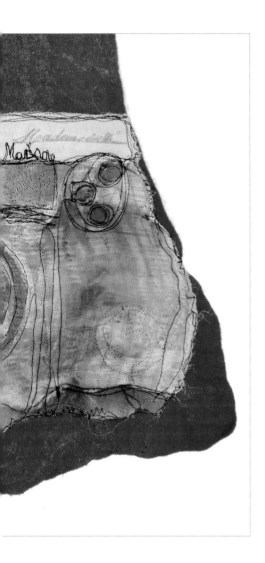

Dress. Polyamide and polypropylene yarn; knitted and heat treated. 2015.

Amy Nguyen
Boston, Massachusetts

I see many parallels to human nature in working with fabric: strength and fragility. The balance that is necessary in life. I seek balance in both the physical and visual texture created from a single expansive piece of white cloth, dyed using ancient techniques, deconstructed, then stitched, pieced, or quilted. Each step informs the next. Kinetic in nature, every piece I make is both sculptural and functional once draped on the body. On the body, this cloth becomes the most intimate art.

I have been exhibiting my hand dyed, intricately stitched clothing nationally since 2007, in juried craft shows such as the Smithsonian Museum show (winner of the first-time exhibitor award), the Philadelphia Museum (winner of *Ornament Magazine*'s "Art to Wear" award), and various American Craft Council shows, where I won the Award of Excellence in San Francisco in 2015.

Quilted Swing Coat. Hand dyed arashi shibori, torn, pieced, quilted silk organza, cotton, fiber reactive dyes, silk thread. 48" × 31". 2013.

Pieced Knit Coat. Hand dyed itajime shibori, hand cut, pieced wool jersey, acid dyes, silk thread. 42" × 30". 2013.

Pleated Wrap. Hand dyed and pleated arashi shibori silk organza, fiber reactive dyes, silk thread. 14" × 7'6". 2013.

Cutwork Swing Coat. Hand dyed itajime shibori, pieced, quilted, hand cut silk organza, cotton, fiber reactive dyes, silk thread. 55" × 48". 2013.

OPPOSITE
LEFT *Long Swing Coat.* Hand dyed itajime shibori, stitched, pieced locally sourced wool, acid dyes, silk thread. 56" × 48". 2013.

RIGHT *Pleated Linen Coat.* Hand dyed and hand stitched nui shibori fine handkerchief linen, fiber reactive dyes, silk thread. 52" × 22". 2013.

Matilda Norberg
Malmö, Skåne Län, Sweden

My work focuses on exploring knit techniques in order to find ways of developing and pushing them forward. When an idea of a knit structure suggests new shapes, silhouettes, and methods of constructing garments, I am exactly where I want to be. The circle is a recurring element in my projects, as well as the pursuit of light, sculptural, and voluminous knitted silhouettes.

With a master's degree in Womenswear Knitwear from Royal College of Art, London, and a bachelor's degree in Textiles from Konstfack University College of Arts, Crafts and Design, Stockholm, as well as schooling in traditional artisan handweaving and embroidery, I have a broad knowledge of material and techniques, although my main interest lies in knits and knitwear. I was awarded the Loro Piana Best Knitwear Collection Award 2015, and I was the First Prize Winner of the Feel the Yarn Competition 2014.

Dress. Polyamide and polypropylene yarn; knitted and heat treated. 2015.

All art images courtesy of Ceen Wahren.

Jacket. Wool/polyamide yarn and
polyurethane foam; knitted. 2015.

Coat. Cashmere/viscose/
polyester/polyamide yarn,
neoprene foam, viscose
jersey fabric; knitted and
fused. 2015.

OPPOSITE
Dress. Silk jersey, spacer
fabric, polyurethane foam;
fused/laminated. 2015.

Artist in *Fairy Floss*.
Photographer: Brett Stanley.

Claire Prebble
Takaka, New Zealand

I live my art. My creativity is integral to me, and I always have ideas! My chosen mediums are sterling silver and copper wire, with gold a new interest, along with silk fabrics, Swarovski crystals, glass beads, and semiprecious stones. I started playing with wire as a child, and something just happened. Wire was the thing; it worked and creativity flowed from my fingers to create both wearable art and jewelry. My wearable art forms are often spoken of as full body jewelry, hence the flow of one to the other.

My technique is one I developed by myself and refined over time. I create a lace and lattice work that can be either wicked or ethereally beautiful.

The intricate forms are entwined, plaited, woven, bound, and stitched. There is no soldering involved. It's the wire, my hands, my heart, my mind, and three pairs of pliers. That's my tool kit.

In 2004, at the age of 18, I was the youngest person to win New Zealand's World of Wearable Art (WOW) Supreme Award and the Reflective Surfaces Award with *Eos*. When not doing my own art or working for clients, I have worked extensively in the film industry starting with *Avatar*, leading on to *The Hobbit* and many other feature films.

Authors' note: Claire Prebble passed away on December 23, 2015.

Lunaria. Stitched, woven, plaited, bound, and beaded silver wire; tea dyed and steam crinkled silk organza, glass beads, and Swarovski crystals. 2003. Photographer: Kaveh Kardan.

▲ *Black Raven.* Stitched and twisted steel tie wire, hard coated with urethane plastic; silk and tulle. Created for the World of Wearable Art Awards. 2007. Photographer: Alessandro Saponi.

► *White.* Stitched, woven, plaited, bound, and beaded silver wire; Swarovski crystals, organza silk. 2012. Photographer: Alessandro Saponi.

OPPOSITE
Eos. Stitched, woven, plaited, bound, and beaded silver and copper wire; silk organza, silk dupion, glass beads, and Swarovski crystals. 2004. Photographer: Simon Godsiff.

Zebedee. Stitched, woven, plaited, bound, and beaded silver wire; organza silk, Swarovski crystals, and Japanese glass beads. 2006.
Photographer: Alessandro Saponi.

OPPOSITE
LEFT *Princess.* Stitched, woven, plaited, bound, and beaded silver wire; sterling silver wire, Swarovski crystals, semi-precious stones, glass beads, and vintage doilies. 2014. Photographer: Brett Stanley.

RIGHT Artist in *Fairy Floss.* Stitched, woven, plaited, bound, and beaded silver wire; silk organza, glass beads, and Swarovski crystals. 2014.
Photographer: Brett Stanley.

Della Reams
Oxford, Ohio

My inspiration comes from cultural symbols and the spiritual characteristics of a culture. I develop contemporary garments utilizing natural fiber yarns and traditional techniques mixed with contemporary manufacturing technology—digital weaving, machine knitting, and digital printing—using symbols from cultures and ethnic and cultural exchange to imbue my work with vitality and spirit. These symbols visually represent the effect of the increased feeling of well-being on the wearer or observer.

Living in the Middle East and traveling around the Eastern Hemisphere inspired me to wander outside the discipline of fashion and look into architecture, interior design, graphic design, and fine arts. With international and interdisciplinary collaborators, I work with graphic design/dresses, furniture/clothing, and painting/fabrics/garments.

I have made garments since I was a child, earned a bachelor's degree in Textiles and Clothing, and had my own apparel business for many years. Since earning an MFA in Textiles from Rhode Island School of Design in 2005, I have integrated the two-dimensional practice of textile design with the three-dimensional perspective of fashion design. My skill in designing and creating original textiles has greatly expanded my ability to design innovative garments.

I show my work internationally in juried exhibitions and have received design awards from the Surface Design Association, ATEXINC (Apparel and Textile Education Xchange), and Cotton Incorporated. I also teach university courses in fashion and textile design and making, as well as in the business of design.

Carla Smoking Jacket and Skirt. Cashmere/silk yarn; digitally designed, machine knitted fabric, hand manipulated pattern shapes, hand crochet, hand and machine sewn. 2009. Photograph by Ahmed El Sayed.

Felicity Dress. One hundred percent bamboo yarn; digitally designed, machine knitted fabric, hand manipulated pattern shapes, hand sewn. 2013. Featuring Felicity Ulmer's monogram in Arabic. Photograph by Hisham Dawoud.

Maryam Dress. Wool/rayon crepe, polyester chenille and stretch yarns, with nylon tulle skirt; digitally designed, machine knitted fabric, hand manipulated pattern shapes, hand and machine sewn. 2011. Featuring Maryam Al Thani's monogram in Arabic.

OPPOSITE
Nada Dress. Wool/rayon crepe yarn; digitally designed, machine knitted fabric, hand manipulated pattern shapes, hand crochet, hand and machine sewn. 2012. Featuring Nada Hammada's monogram in Arabic.

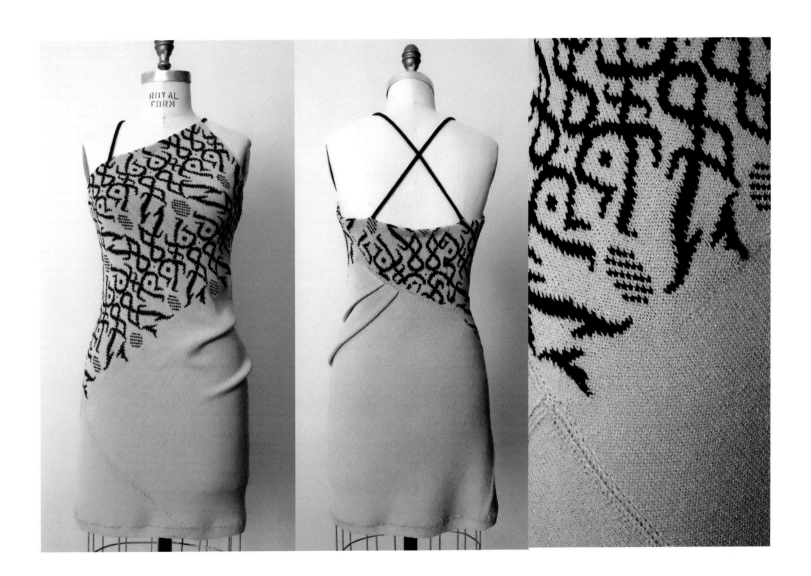

Artist in *Forest Dweller*. Fabric, netting, embroidery floss, thread, and mixed media; hand and free-motion machine embroidery, sewing. 2014.

Leisa Rich
Atlanta, Georgia

I am a modern day creative archaeologist and experimentalist. I apply fine art, craft, and fiber art techniques to repurpose the old and reenvision the new.

After receiving a BFA in Fibers in 1982, my first job was as a wearable art designer for an international design house in Toronto. I then branched off to sell my own hats, jewelry, and clothing creations, which were featured on television, in magazines, and in 125 stores. I received a Bachelor of Education in Art in 1993 and an MFA in Fibers in 2007. In the late 1990s, I returned to making non-functional art but am occasionally compelled to do art-to-wear when it coincides with an idea.

Forest Dweller represents fecund growth and the overtaking of the human body by nature, albeit forms of manufactured natural elements conceived and brought to fruition by human ingenuity. Ripped fabrics meander and sprout as roots and branches, and hand embroidery references spider webs: strong yet delicate.

OPPOSITE AND ABOVE
Catcall: Bootycall. Recycled plastic foot booties, vinyl, acrylic
paint; sewn, painted, assembled. Installation. 2015.

Snapped. Recycled snap tape, fabric, foam. Sewn. 2014.

OPPOSITE
Birds of a Feather Falling from the Nest. Heat formed fabric, recycled wedding gown, thread and mixed media; heat application, free-motion machine embroidery, sewing. Installation. 2013.

Courtesy of Ryan Macchione.

K. Riley
Havertown, Pennsylvania

My training and specialties are in textile and apparel design, illustration, and costume history. As a starting point for a body of work, I choose a theme and a technique to explore. I draw inspiration from a wide range of interests: medieval reliquaries, Persian miniatures, and Japanese kimonos to name a few. My techniques have included hand painting, stenciling, stitching, and block printing.

My most recent work is botanically inspired, featuring a selection of insects and plants, and I've chosen linoleum block printing to apply the surface design. I design, illustrate, and painstakingly hand carve each linoleum block, using multiple blocks for each individual garment printing. All garment sections are printed before construction. I layer prints and colors to get the desired effect, carefully considering all the garment details as I print.

My silhouettes are drawn from costume history. I translate shapes and details from the past to create a contemporary garment. My goal is to create a beautifully constructed garment with unique design and impeccable craftsmanship.

All art images courtesy of Peter Groesbeck.

Jacket with Fish. Hand block printed using hand carved linoleum blocks. Wool suiting, textile paint. 24" × 23". 2011.

Kimono Jacket with Dragonfly. Hand block printed with hand carved linoleum blocks. Silk taffeta. 30" × 24". 2015.

Draped Vest with Plants. Hand block printed using hand carved linoleum blocks. Wool suiting with silk taffeta trim, textile paint. 38" × 27". 2011.

Sleeveless Kimono with Honeybee. Hand block printed using hand carved linoleum blocks. Silk taffeta, textile paint. 24" × 23". 2015.

Jacket with Dragonfly and Plants. Hand block printed using hand carved linoleum blocks. Silk taffeta with silk organza trim, textile paint. 24" × 27". 2011.

Kimono Jacket with Crickets.
Hand block printed using hand
carved linoleum blocks. Rayon
ponte double knit, textile paints.
30" × 21". 2015.

Carole Simcox
*Salt Spring Island,
British Columbia, Canada*

I find myself drawn to natural fibers and creating beautiful works of art with intriguing textures. There is an exhilaration that I get, starting with some roving, bits of fiber, and a concept, reworking everything until the finished art materializes. With each piece of work, I try for something distinctly expressive and magical, whether it is something abstract or realistic.

My goal is to have the beauty of nature reflected in my work. I currently live in one of the most beautiful places in the world, Salt Spring Island, where the ocean, wildlife, birds, and forests provide an abundance of inspiration.

Renaissance. Wet felt mosaic jacket. Merino wool, mulberry silks, ribbons, crocheted flowers, cords, embroidery threads, fabric, oatmeal wool, prefelt, vintage buttons. 28.5" × 20". 2013.
Photo by Kristine Mayes.

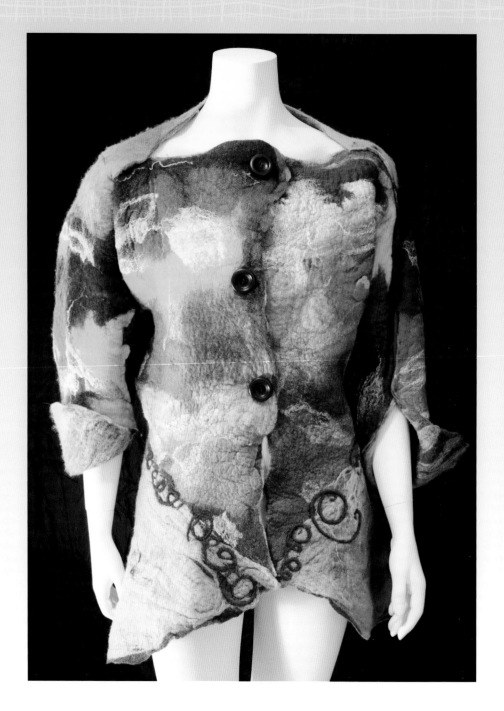

▲ *Autumn.* Wet felt cowl. Merino wool in orange, yellow, dark burgundy, and turquoise, hand dyed mulberry silk hankies and sea foam mulberry silk strands. 13" (doubled) × 27". 2012. Photo by Kristine Mayes.

► *Progressions.* Wet felt dress. Warrior flash swirl llama, ecru merino wool, merino tussah silk wool, beads, vintage rhinestone and shell buttons, Falkland wool. 28" × 14.5". 2012.

Flowers. Nuno felt dress. Silk chiffon, mulberry silk, pieces of silk, thread, merino wools, flower trims. 30" × 18". 2013.

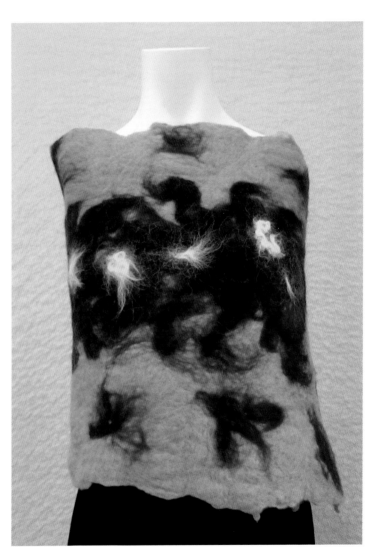

In Pinks. Seamless wet felt tank top. Merino wool in two
tonal pinks and peacock mulberry silk. 19.25" × 39". 2012.
Photo by Kristine Mayes.

Alpaca Curls. Seamless wet felt shawl. Merino wool in lilac and
eggplant and Alpaca ecru natural curls. 47.25" × 17". 2011.

Anne Vincent
Atlanta, Georgia

My handmade textiles result from my lifelong love of fiber. Wool and/or silk combine with alpaca, linen, cotton, ribbons, yarns, beads, sequins, and other fibers in works of wearable art.

I use hand dyeing, shibori techniques, felting, nuno felting, and needle felting to explore the tactile and visual characteristics of these materials. The results vary from comfortably casual to fabulously formal. Inspiration comes from a wide range of sources: the natural world of plants and animals, historical textiles, my garden, snowflakes, water, and stone.

Silver Lining Wrap. Hand dyed silk and merino wool, with printed silk chiffon and silk yarns. Approximately 30" × 7'8".

◄ *Turquoise Russet Coat.* Hand dyed silks, merino wool, printed silk chiffons seamlessly nuno felted. Reversible. Photograph courtesy of Mark Krause.

▼ *White Shrug.* Silk organza and merino wool; hand felted. 66" × 44". Photograph courtesy of Mark Krause.

Itajime and Arashi Shibori Wrap "Red." Hand dyed silk habotai;
folded, clamped, discharged, vat dyed, and pole wrapped.

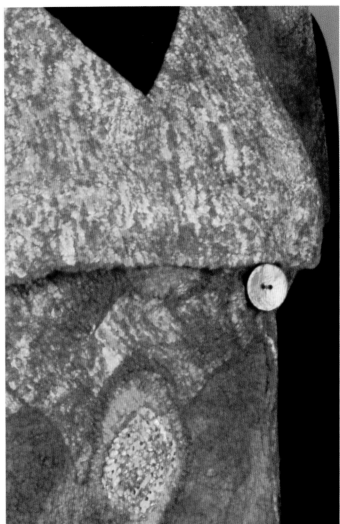

Red Flame Vest. Hand dyed silks, Merino wool, printed silk chiffons, silk and wool embellishments; nuno felted seamlessly.

Photo by Jansen Wendlandt.

Rebecca Wendlandt
Davis, California

Joy, beauty, vibrancy, and life are qualities that I value and seek to express in my art. I love exploring color, texture, shape, and movement. When I am working on a design, I start with the human body and build out from it. I create sculptural forms that flow in and out of the body's natural silhouette, complementing the body and never completely obscuring it. Body movement offers an exciting dimension to the design process, creating an avenue through which my art can transform from one moment to the next.

The body is always my first inspiration, but certainly not my only one. Nature is a consistent source of inspiration. The enormous variety of designs in the natural world never ceases to provide new thrilling discoveries and ideas. Additionally, my work is often influenced by history and culture through which my art is given context and infused with a broader view of civilization. At times, my inspiration is more abstract and simple, consisting of geometry, color, and the human body.

I seek to achieve both a striking silhouette from a distance and a deep, rich, detailed surface up close. To accomplish this, I combine different materials and manipulate fabric surfaces through various methods such as stitching, fusing, cutting, heat setting, dyeing, and painting.

OPPOSITE AND ABOVE
Water Dancers. Silk, polyester, thermoplastic fabric, wire, boning,
paint, dye; machine and hand stitching, heat setting, fusing,
cutting, painting, and dyeing. 6' 8" × 30" × 21". 2014.
Photo by Todd & Barbara Photography.

Dinobryon Mystic. Silk organza, wool roving, boning, wire, dye, paint; machine and hand stitching, dyeing, and painting. 70" × 40" × 40". 2013. Photo by Todd & Barbara Photography.

Exuberant. Silk dupioni, organza, heavy fusible interfacing, and thread; machine and hand stitching, cutting, and fusing. 34" × 29" × 23". 2008. Photo by Ray Johnston.

Laverne Zabielski
Monticello, Kentucky

Dressing up,
wearing art,
changes your stance.
It is a power tool.
It makes a statement.

Not so much by wearing the latest fashion, but by the
way you layer what you have, whether it's brand new or
make-do. With conscious attention to textures and palette,
you create rhythm and balance. Poetry.

You say

I know who I am. I know what I'm doing.

When I see dressed up,
in Sunday best, painted blue jeans or art to wear
I see soft.
I see caring and tenderness.
I see take a stand.
I see power.
I see

I know who I am. I know what I'm doing.

Growing up, shopping for fabric with my mother was a peak experience. It made perfect sense that I created clothing when I learned the shibori technique for dyeing fabric. I always use at least three colors when applying dye in order to create movement, texture, and harmony. Instead of buying patterns, I tear my dyed fabric into strips and panels. Arturo Alonzo Sandoval taught me the arashi shibori technique. Lanette Freitag, inventor of the FeltLOOM, taught me felting.

OPPOSITE
Caftan Jacket. Shibori dyed, pole wrapped, pieced with fringe edge, silk devore and crepe. 2015. Courtesy M.S. Rezny.

Eco Topper. Felted on FeltLOOM. Kentucky wool, silk, upcycled shibori dyed merino, and silk. 2015. Courtesy M.S. Rezny.

Eco Poncho. Felted on FeltLOOM. Upcycled shibori dyed merino and silk. 2015. Courtesy M.S. Rezny.

Circle Vest. Felted on FeltLOOM. Merino
and silk, shibori dyed, pole wrapped. 2015.
Courtesy Anna Esposito.

FOREWORD

Jewelry and Fiber Art   *Margery Goldberg*

What is fiber art, and how does jewelry fit into that realm?

Wikipedia states, "Fiber art refers to fine art whose material consists of natural or synthetic fiber and other components, such as fabric or yarn. It focuses on the materials and on the manual labor on the part of the artist as part of the work's significance, and prioritizes aesthetic value over utility." Like the contributors to Wikipedia, I thought of "fiber" as cotton and wool, thread and yarn, cloth, rugs, and blankets, and "fiber art" as using these materials and making them into something beautiful—into art—through techniques such as quilting, weaving, embroidery, needlepoint, knitting, and crocheting. Further, using the above definition, I would not consider jewelry an art form, because, by definition, jewelry has utility through being worn for adornment.

Well, open your mind, because this book explodes this traditional definition. It proves that fiber art can come from metal, paper, glass, and many other materials besides the traditional ones. It questions the definition of art itself. These jewelers *are* artists. They push the boundaries of fiber and art in every direction. Some use traditional materials in an untraditional way; others do just the opposite. Some create jewelry as sculpture; some make the wearer into sculpture. Basically, they all break the rules for fiber, art, and jewelry in some way, and I love it.

So, forget what you think jewelry should look like: most of the jewelry in this book defines adornment in the broadest of terms. There are pieces that look more like sculpture than jewelry, such as Sayumi Yokouchi's pieces that, in her words, "are unique creatures

of intricate ornamentation and intimate patterns of organisms, which seem to resemble the community we humans inhabit." Małgosia Kalińska says, "I deliberately limit the participation of rhythmic structures to black and white. This allows me to differentiate absorption of light, which as a concentrated or dispersed energy becomes a play on matter and space." Tina Lazzarine uses the collar to demonstrate the complex identity of woman as both oppressed and empowered, while Jera Lodge says that her jewelry "is inspired by my love for adornment, an interest in patterns and line, and a sense of functionality."

Forget what you think about fiber as material: much of the jewelry in his book defines fiber in the broadest of terms. You will find paper, copper wire, fishing line, glass, and Velcro (yes, Velcro), as well as traditional fibers such as cotton, synthetic fabric, silk organza, merino wool, and other materials. You will find that some of the art looks like one material when it is really another, such as Mariko Kusumoto's work that looks as if it is made of glass, yet is really made of fabric, and Yong Joo Kim's pieces, which look like felt or other fabric, and are made of Velcro. Many artists use similar materials but express it with a completely different aesthetic, such as Luis Acosta's layered paper pieces based on the repetition of an interesting form versus Ania Gilmore's, which show her interest "in creating pieces that can be changed or adjusted in the process while the basic fiber content remains present. Since nothing in life is permanent, the idea of deliberately working with impermanence of paper seems very natural." Nontraditional is the name of the game here.

And . . . forget what you think about art: art is no longer the painting on your wall, no longer the sculpture in your garden, no longer what you see at a museum. It is what you see and buy at a craft show; it is what you find at an art gallery; it is whatever has an aesthetic value beyond utility, beyond the classic art forms, and way beyond what you were taught in school. Art is jewelry like this!

As a gallery owner and artist, I am used to people coming to my gallery with preset notions about art, but, instead, they find things they have never seen or even dreamt of. This includes jewelry. I sell jewelry. I have seen thousands of jewelers over the more than thirty-five years that I have been a gallery owner. Yet, my mouth still drops open when I look at the work of the artists in this book. The fiber art jewelers in *Artistry in Fiber, Vol. 3: Wearable Art* fulfill the primary quality I look for in selecting artists and art for my gallery—they are artgasmic.

I would like to acknowledge the editorial talents of my friend Sharon Leiser, an appreciator of arts, an excellent writer, and a lawyer.

Luis Acosta
Utrecht, The Netherlands

I am of Argentine-Dutch descent, and graduated in 1988 from the textile department of the Gerrit Rietveld Academy in Amsterdam. As a textile and jewelry designer, I am particularly interested in forms. Once a form is found, I enlarge or repeat it. Then I concentrate on using the possibilities of that form as a basis to develop a design. I work with both shapes and color: the first gives dimension to the design while the second provides warmth. One way of doing this, is to "play" with a shape and several layers of different colored paper or paper thread, which sometimes gives rise to an intriguing hybridization, conjuring up the impression of something plaited.

I have participated in group and individual exhibitions in most European countries, Argentina, the United States, Japan, and South Korea, earning an Honorable Mention for Contemporary Jewellery at ENJOIA'T Barcelona in 2010. My works are in the Museum of Arts and Design (New York City), and the Costume Museum (Buenos Aires); the CODA Museum, the Centre of Fine Arts, and the Textile Museum, all in the Netherlands; as well as in private collections worldwide. I have also curated and served on the jury of several exhibitions in Spain and the Netherlands and I teach courses in South America, Europe, and the United States on design for woven fabrics and paper jewelry.

Stairs. Six stitched layers of paper. 2.16" diameter × 0.78". 2012.

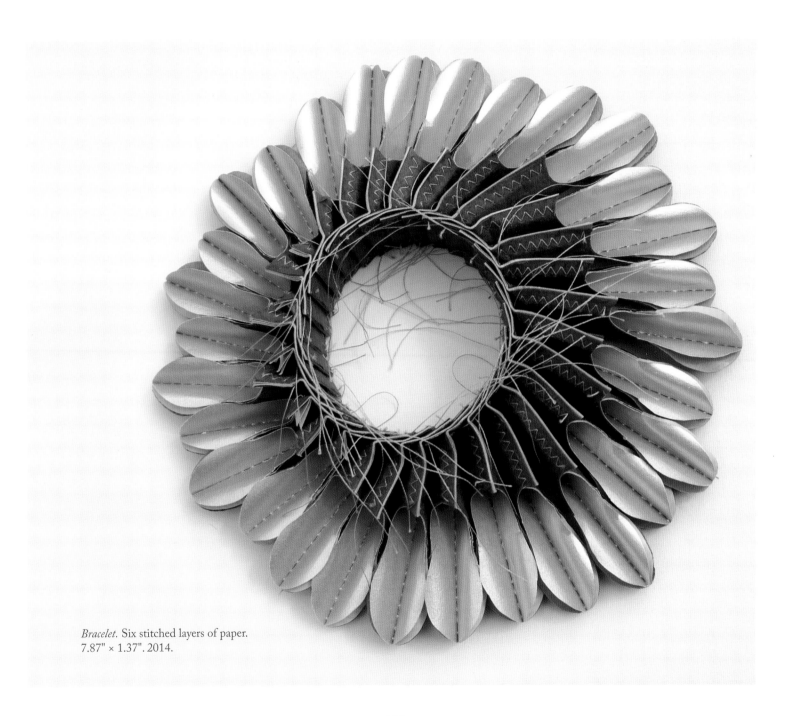

Bracelet. Six stitched layers of paper.
7.87" × 1.37". 2014.

Bracelet. Six stitched layers of paper. 6.29" × 1.96". 2014.

OPPOSITE
LEFT *Quipus* (knot). Stitched paper, thread. 19.68" diameter. 2013.

RIGHT Six stitched layers of paper. 15.74" diameter. 2015.

Weaving embodies rhythm, balance, and order to create a dynamic equilibrium of structure, pattern, and form that is integral to the human experience. My jewelry explores the beauty of symmetry revolving around the seamless continuity of a circle. Inspired by mandalas, I express the elegance of geometry through graceful forms of metal and monofilament, merging the ancient, current, and future. Through the integration of weaving and goldsmithing, the durability and strength of metal combine with the luminosity and flexibility of plastic. I assign a new application to a traditional technique, turning double-weave cloth into dimensional-weave jewelry.

Anastasia Azure
Providence, Rhode Island

Coaxial Providence. Sterling and fine silver, fishing line, and pearls. 2009.

All art images courtesy of Hap Sakwa.

Recursive. Brass, copper, sterling silver, and fishing line. 2009.

Victoria Garnet Pendant. Sterling and fine silver, garnet, and fishing line. 2009.

Angle Up Close. Patina copper and fishing line. 2006.

Accentuating Focus. Brass, copper, and fishing line. 2008.

Photo by Robin Dreyer.

David K. Chatt
Midway, Kentucky

I have spent thirty years stitching tiny bits of glass one to the other in unexpected ways and by unexpected hands. I am a fifty-six-year-old, six-foot-five, white guy; not who comes to mind when one thinks of beadwork. A younger version of myself worried about the fact that I was inexplicably drawn to a medium so laden with cultural and gender-based bias. More truthfully, others worried, and I worried that I should worry. I no longer do.

My work tells of the odd world I inhabit, a place that is more interesting than comfortable. I limit my use of color and use beads as a reductive medium rather than as embellishment. I am interested in the transformation that occurs when seemingly innocuous objects are placed in unfamiliar environments. I look for objects that hold meaning and can be seen anew when covered in tiny glass beads and meticulous needlework: for example, plastic soldiers are placed in the hands of children without fully considering the consequence; when employed as jewelry, the subject matter becomes much more controversial. An object covered in this way is now less that object and more the place where that object once was, like a memory held in time and space.

In 2007, the Bellevue Arts Museum in Washington honored me with a retrospective look at my career entitled *Two Hands, Twenty Years, and a Billion Beads*. I am a former Penland Resident Artist (2008–2011); in 2015, I was awarded a North Carolina Arts Council fellowship.

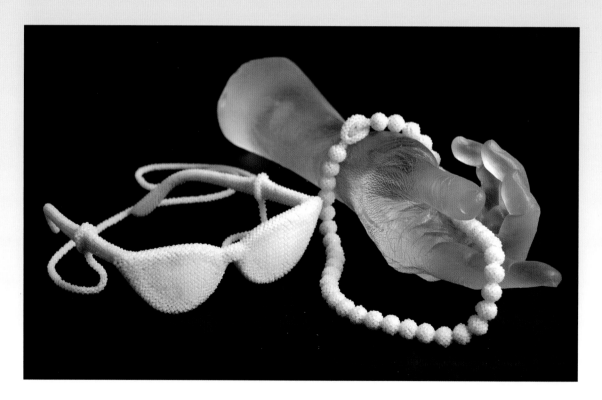

Glasses and Pearls. Glasses and knotted beads covered in sewn glass beads and thread. 2014. Photo by Dana Moore.

Artillery Necklace. Glass beads, thread, and found objects. 2016. Photo by Mercedes Jelinek.

Scissors, Pen, Waiter's Knife.
Objects covered in sewn glass beads
and thread, ball chains. 2016.
Photo by Mercedes Jelinek.

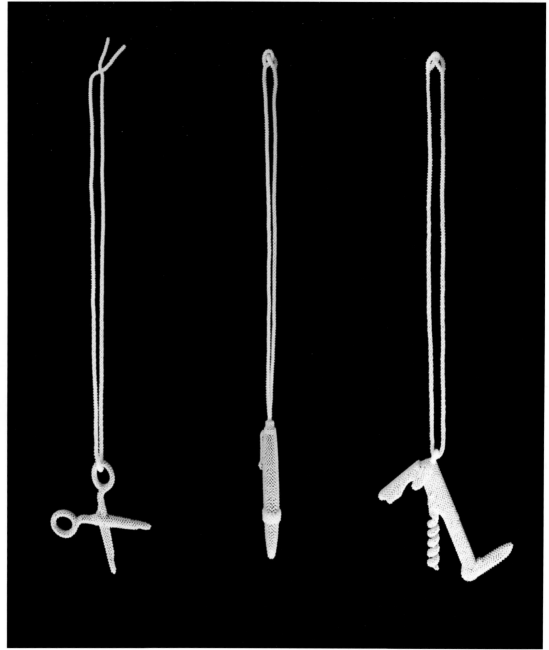

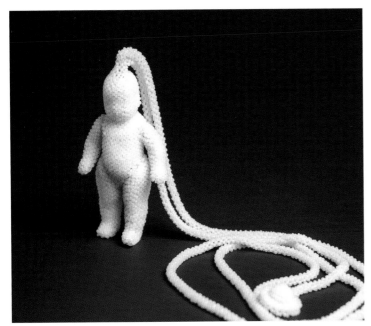

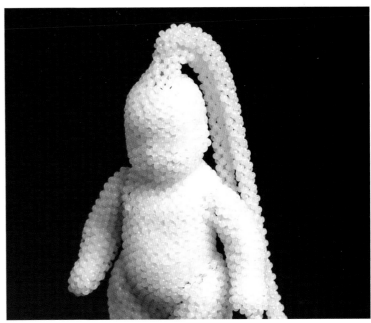

▲ *Baby Doll Necklace.* Antique doll covered in sewn glass beads and thread. Doll: 3" tall. 2014. Photo by Dana Moore.

◄ *Black Dog Necklace.* Plastic toy dog covered in sewn glass beads and thread, ball chain. 2015. Photo by Kathryn Gremley.

Evy Edelman
New York, New York

Prior to becoming a goldsmith, I was a designer for the home furnishing industry working with various textiles, including crewel fabric. I used this education as a stepping stone into the world of one-of-a-kind pieces of jewelry incorporating gold, gemstones, and granulation. I have always thought of the technique of granulation as similar to that of embroidery, even though one is made out of metal and the other is made out of threads.

I am fortunate to be able to travel to Bangkok, Hong Kong, and other exotic locales to seek out and find the unusual and precious gemstones and pearls featured in my work. A sparkling gemstone speaks its own language and conveys to me the best way to showcase its natural beauty. Once I envision the design, I create it, in gold or silver, using various jewelry techniques.

My distinctive one-of-a-kind pieces are a result of a creative drive that fulfills my need to never be bored when at my workbench. My goal is to continue to evolve each and every time I sit down at my workbench and create a completely unique and original piece each and every time.

Golden Moth Pin/Pendant.
Handcrafted in 22K gold with four granulated wings, aquamarine body, South Sea pearl head, and diamonds. 4" wide. 2012.

All photos courtesy of Robert Edelman.

Shard Necklace. Hand fabricated granulation in 22K gold design representing shards of broken pottery; unique aquamarine slices accented with tourmaline and iolite gemstones. 2012.

Silver Topaz Pendant. 125-carat sandblasted natural stone set in an 18K basket bezel wrapped with a fine silver handwoven chain. 2013.

Golden Bugs 2 A-Lite. Pendant with two handmade 22K gold granulated bugs with tourmaline bodies, and peridot and topaz heads, mounted on 2.75" × 1.5" Labradorite stone framed in 18K gold, with 22K gold handwoven 18" chain. 2015.

Empress Rubellite Necklace. Four strands of hand fabricated
18K links woven into a chain framing a 19.73-carat natural
stone with 0.49-carat diamond. 2014.

Arline M. Fisch
San Diego, California

My work in metal began in the mid-1950s, when the interest was in clean lines and plain surfaces, and was reinforced by a year of study in Denmark. My personal interest in jewelry, however, was based upon studies of ancient cultures where the richness of surface and the drama of scale were so imposing. These inspired me to explore many techniques that were not so much in favor: chasing and repoussé, mixing of metals, and materials such as feathers and leather. My strongest exploration all through the 1960s was that of scale: full-length body ornaments, headgear, and sleeve-like arm ornaments.

In the 1970s, I began to use textile structures—weaving, braiding, and knitting—primarily in fine silver, which led to two books on the subject, as well as a large body of work. I continue to explore and expand many different textile structures, now often using color-coated copper wire. I am still intrigued by large and dramatic jewelry for which textile structures are ideally suited because they produce soft and transparent forms, which drape and encircle the body and are comfortable to wear.

Bracelet and Glove. Machine knit coated copper, hand knit fine silver.
5" diameter × 20". 1999. Collection of Renwick Gallery, Washington, DC.
Photo by William Gullette.

Pink and Silver Circles Necklace. Machine knit, coated copper, fine
silver crochet, and sterling. 14" outer diameter × 6" to 8" tubes. 2005.
Photo by William Gullette.

Knit Bracelets. Coated copper wire; machine knit, crochet edge. Various sizes: 5" × 3" to 6". 2009. Photo by William Gullette.

◄ *Pale Green Collar and Brooch Necklace.* Coated copper wire, sterling, pearls; spool knit. 3.5" × 14" band; 4.5" diameter brooch. 2015.

▼ *Lace Halo Collar.* Fine silver, sterling, pearls, crochet, and hairpin lace. 9" × 10". 2005.

Courtesy of Jerry Gilmore.

Ania Gilmore
*Boston, Massachusetts
& Poland*

I love paper!

The secret of papermaking migrated in the third century from China, to Vietnam, and Tibet, and by the fourth century to Korea and Japan. *Joomchi* is a traditional Korean technique of felting mulberry fibers (Hanji). The process is quite meditative and joyful, even though it requires a lot of energy and strength. Joomchi enables me to play with the structure, to alter the properties of the fibers from smooth leather-like to strong textural paper. I am interested in creating pieces that can be changed or adjusted in the process while the basic fiber content remains present. Since nothing in life is permanent, the idea of deliberately working with the impermanence of paper seems very natural.

I received a BFA with honors in Graphic Design from Massachusetts College of Art and Design; I studied printmaking, book art, and fibers at the Rhode Island School of Design, the School of the Museum of Fine Arts in Boston, and at the Haystack Mountain School of Crafts in Maine. My work has been exhibited in museums and galleries in the United States, Europe, Australia, and Korea and is included in numerous public and private collections.

Released to Joy Joomchi Necklace.
Korean mulberry paper, thread.
18" (extendable). 2015.

➤ *Wanderer 46 Joomchi Brooch.* Korean mulberry paper. 3.5" × 2.5". 2015.

▼ *Wanderer 79 Joomchi Brooch.* Korean mulberry paper. 3" × 4". 2015.

◄ *Wanderer 88 Joomchi Brooch.* Korean mulberry paper. 6" × 0.8". 2015.

Maja Houtman
Utrecht, The Netherlands

I was educated as a gold- and silversmith at the Vakschool in Schoonhoven; after an apprenticeship in Chatham, Ontario, I graduated in 1988 in both disciplines. In a suburb of Utrecht, in the center of the Netherlands, I found my first job as a repairer in a mainstream jewelry shop.

In 1992, I made a career switch and accepted an appointment as assay master at the Dutch Assay Office in Gouda. For over ten years, I assessed almost everything made of platinum, gold, and silver that was sold in the Netherlands. I then started to work as an artist goldsmith and over fifteen years have developed my own style of wirework, which has evolved into objects, bowls, and exclusive pieces of jewelry.

Phoenix Egg. Ring. 18K yellow gold filigree, rutile quartz, and coral. 1.96" × 1.81" × 1.69". Courtesy of the Bundesverband der Edelstein- und Diamantindustrie e.V.

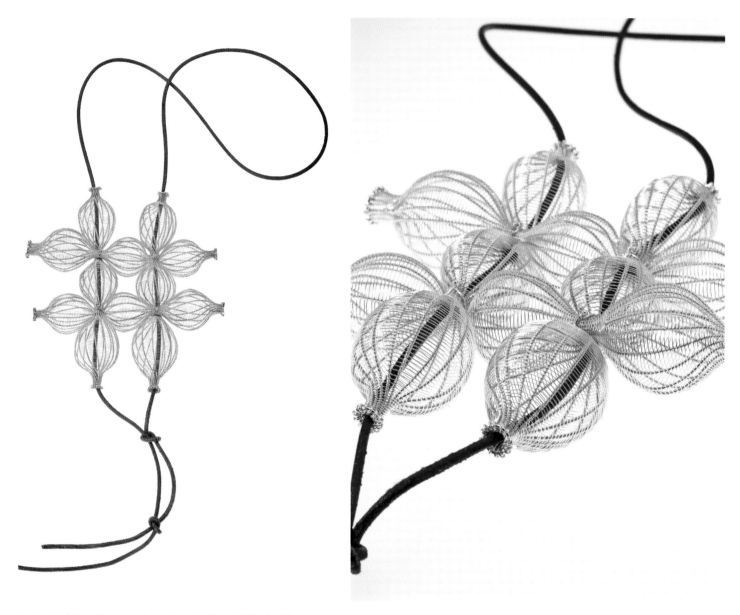

Bobelo Kaptilo. Silver filigree and pendant. 2.95" × 2.95" × 1.18".
2012. Courtesy of Albertine Dijkema, A10design.

◄ *Rosa Krakkerboller*. Chain, filigree, amethyst, and spinel. 23.62" × 0.7" × 1.96". 2014. Courtesy of Albertine Dijkema, A10design.

▼ *Hundo Rosa*. Brooch. Silver filigree. 3.14" × 3.14" × 1.57". Courtesy of Maan Limburg.

◄ and ► *Tetteren aan Tafel (Hollering at the Table)*. Detail shown at right. Ring. Silver filigree and moss agate. 2.55" × 2.16" × 1.77". 2013. Courtesy of Albertine Dijkema, A10design. Made to commemorate the Peace Treaty of Utrecht in 1713, depicting the delegates around the oval table they used.

Carol and Jean-Pierre Hsu

Berkeley Springs,
West Virginia

In the late 1970s, we developed a line of jewelry using combinations of sterling, gold, copper, brass, and nickel. Fabric and clothing influenced our work, but we were searching for a more fiber-like appearance as well as ways to color metal with chemicals, heat, and other techniques.

We purchased a rolling mill in 1980 to texture sheet metals with fabrics to give them varied surfaces. We soon began working with aluminum, which we combine with any possible fabric that can hold up against the powerful pressure of the rolling mill: woven shower curtains, citrus fruit bags, horse feed bags, my parent's living room curtains, and lace. Following this, we anodize in eighteen vibrant colors. The infinite array of combinations and wide variety of textures each express the colors differently. We then hand cut, form, and finish all parts after which most of our jewelry is pinned together with rivets made individually of thin sterling wire.

Aluminum is one of the most ubiquitous materials in the world, used in almost every industry. We enjoy the challenge of creating uncommon works of art for everyday use with a common material.

RIGHT *Marikoi Earrings.*
Anodized aluminum with freshwater pearls. 4" × 2". 2007.

FAR RIGHT *706 Earrings.*
Anodized aluminum. 2.75" × 1".
2006.

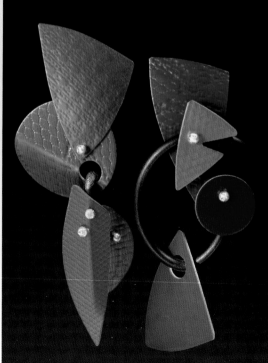

RIGHT *Purple Pin*. Anodized aluminum. 4.5" × 3" × 0.5". 2016.

FAR RIGHT *Tarka Pin*. Anodized aluminum. 2" × 2.25". 2012.

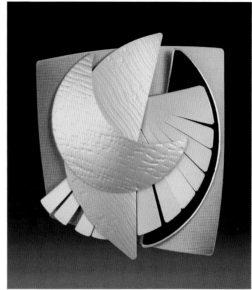

Param Necklace. Anodized aluminum on rubber cords. 3.5" × 5.25" × 0.75". 2014.

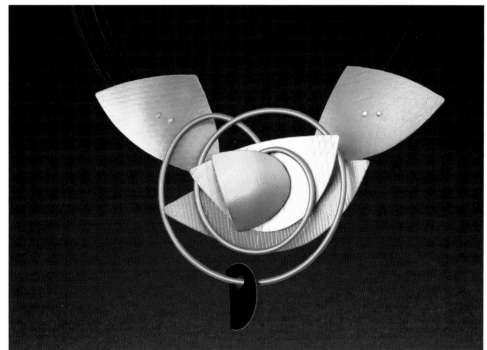

Małgosia Kalińska
Szczecin, Poland

In my creative work, I shift between jewelry and painting.

My disagreement with the haste and ubiquitous excess of modern life is pushing me towards minimalism, harmony, and slowness. These values define the direction for my actions.

In my work I express what concerns the present, even if I am referring to the past or to memories. When exploring purely aesthetic issues, I deliberately limit the participation of rhythmic structures to black and white. This allows me to differentiate absorption of light, which as a concentrated or dispersed energy becomes a play on matter and space. My main materials are foil, silk fabric and cotton, paper, pulp, polymer, and silver, which when are treated accordingly, allow me to create my own language of expression.

No Title No. 1. Necklace. Oxidized silver and plastic bags. 5.9" × 19.68" diameter. 2011.

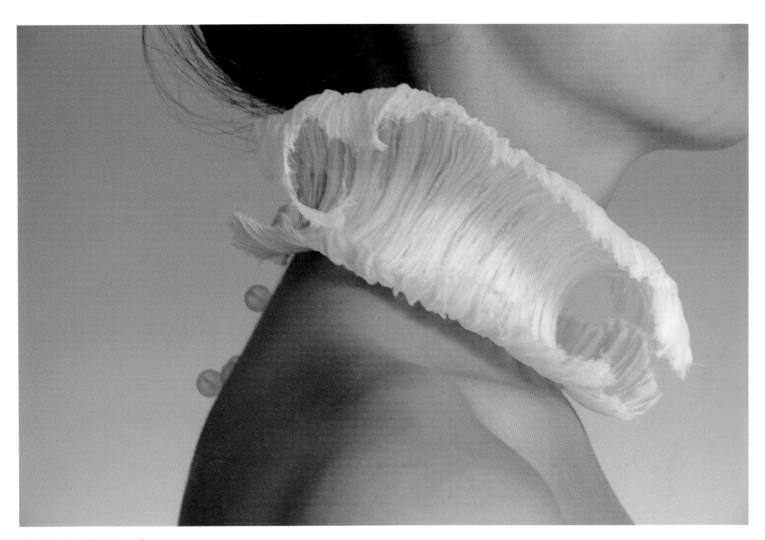

No Title No. 2. Necklace. Organza cotton,
glass, and silver. 3.54" × 11.81". 2010.

No Title No. 3. Necklace. Organza cotton and silver. 1.77" × 3.54". 2010.

No Title No. 4. Brooch. Paper, silver, polymer clay, and paper. 3.14" × 3.14". 2011.

No Title No. 5. Brooch. Paper and silver. 2.75" × 5.51".
2016.

Photo by XianXiu (Heesoo Kim).

Yong Joo Kim
Seoul, South Korea &
Providence, Rhode Island

What does it mean for us to "survive"? For me, making art is a way of exploring this simple yet complicated question. I focus primarily on a single material of choice: hook and loop fasteners. Two reasons inspired my choice to create jewelry out of an inexpensive material often considered unattractive and mundane: it would keep material costs down; and it would challenge my ability to survive in a field known for its use of attractive and precious materials.

What I have since learned is that to survive the creative process we must continue to feel alive without getting stuck and giving up. To do this, we must be able to embrace, respond to, and overcome a variety of unpleasant surprises. When we can do this, we often end up with something that defies our imagination and provides us with experiences of surprise, inspiration, and beauty.

Seven years into this journey, I am grateful to have received both the Society of Arts and Crafts (SAC) and NICHE awards, to have taught at Rhode Island School of Design (RISD), and to have been a featured speaker at the Society of North American Goldsmiths (SNAG) and Sculpture Objects Functional Art and Design (SOFA).

Crossing the Chasm Series. Necklace. Hook-and-loop fasteners, thread, and sterling silver. 10.6" × 18.5" × 1.9". 2016.

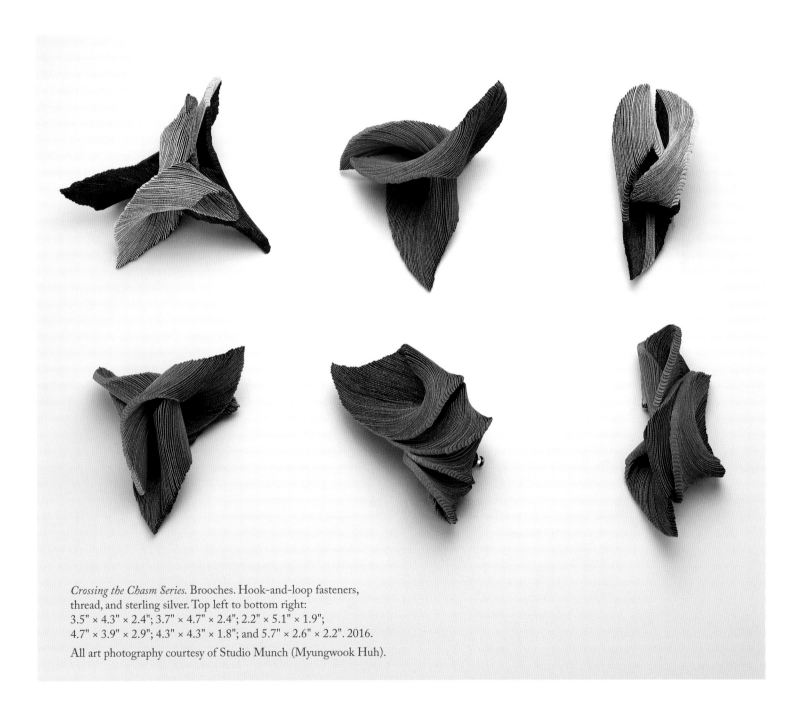

Crossing the Chasm Series. Brooches. Hook-and-loop fasteners,
thread, and sterling silver. Top left to bottom right:
3.5" × 4.3" × 2.4"; 3.7" × 4.7" × 2.4"; 2.2" × 5.1" × 1.9";
4.7" × 3.9" × 2.9"; 4.3" × 4.3" × 1.8"; and 5.7" × 2.6" × 2.2". 2016.

All art photography courtesy of Studio Munch (Myungwook Huh).

In Light of Space II. Bracelets.
Hook-and-loop fasteners and thread.
Left to right: (top) 5.9" × 4.7" × 5.1";
4.3" × 3.9" × 4.3"; 6.7" × 5.1" × 5.1";
(bottom) 8.3" × 4.3" × 4.3";
4.7" × 4.3" × 4.3". 2014.

Transitions in Red XII. Necklace.
Hook-and-loop fasteners, thread, and
sterling silver. 8.7" × 9.4" × 1.6". 2016.

Photo: Steve Mann.

Lisa Klakulak
Asheville, North Carolina

My first exploits in jewelry were made by intertwining the tiniest of glass seed beads into cylindrical walls amassed into hollow sculptural forms. This adornment inspired my undergraduate pursuit of metalsmithing, although I incorporated fiber materials and techniques into all my class projects, if not completely covering my metal forms in beadwork. It became obvious that fiber was to be my BFA focus. Twenty years later, time has revealed that human adornment would remain central to my visual expression, albeit in felt, rather than beads.

Similar to beading, wet felting is also an amassing of tiny elements, filaments of animal fiber. Although beads can be woven to bezel an object, I find felting has a more nurturing, swaddling action as it shrinks down to embrace an object such as broken coral or shell. With a slightly divergent technique, I am able to envelop metal wire armature in extremely thin, high-shrinkage felt, which becomes taut, literally like a protective skin stretched over a skeletal system. In addition to this binding, blanketing power of wool, the individual fibers can also be coerced through other substrates, and this differential shrinkage of wool fiber and silk fabric, for example, develops unique textures. I use this process to "glue" layers of transparent fabric into pockets to include objects such as beach glass.

Felt's supple surface is more than receptive to stitching, and I use the tension of a sewing machine's stitch to compact the air spaces remaining in the felt, stiffening the fabric as well as creating an embossed surface texture. Shrinkage and constriction are my process, yet my relationship with wool is ever expanding, and I am able to work far more intricate detail with a stitch than I ever was interweaving the tiniest of glass seed beads.

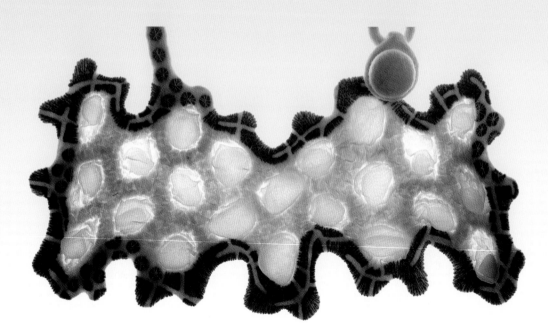

RIGHT AND OPPOSITE
Hardened. Backlit detail at right. Chest piece. Merino wool, silk fabric, repurposed beach glass; needle and wet felting techniques, free-motion machine embroidered, hand stitched. 10.75" × 7.75" × 0.75". 2015. Photo: Steve Mann.

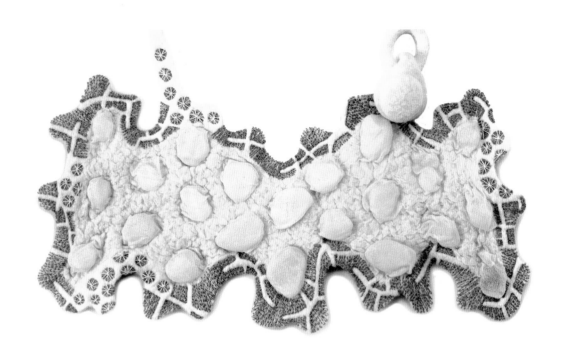

➤ *Neckpiece.* Merino wool, novelty yarn, cotton and waxed linen thread, stainless steel armature; needle and wet felting techniques, free-motion machine embroidered, hand stitched. 7.5" × 6.5" × 0.75". 2015. Photo: Stewart Stokes.

▼ *Earrings.* Merino wool fiber, repurposed coral, cotton and raw silk thread, sterling silver hoops; needle and wet felting techniques, hand stitched. 2" × 1.25" × 1.4". 2015. Photo: Steve Mann.

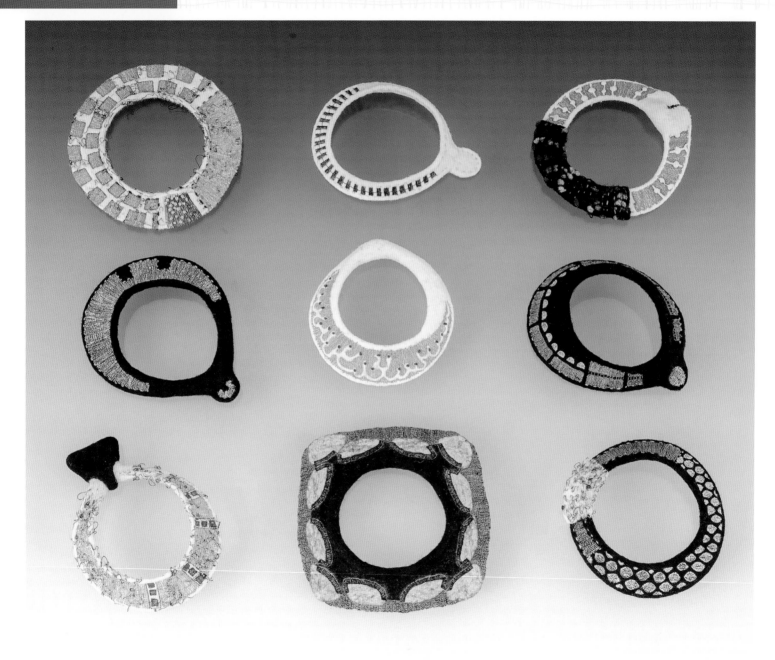

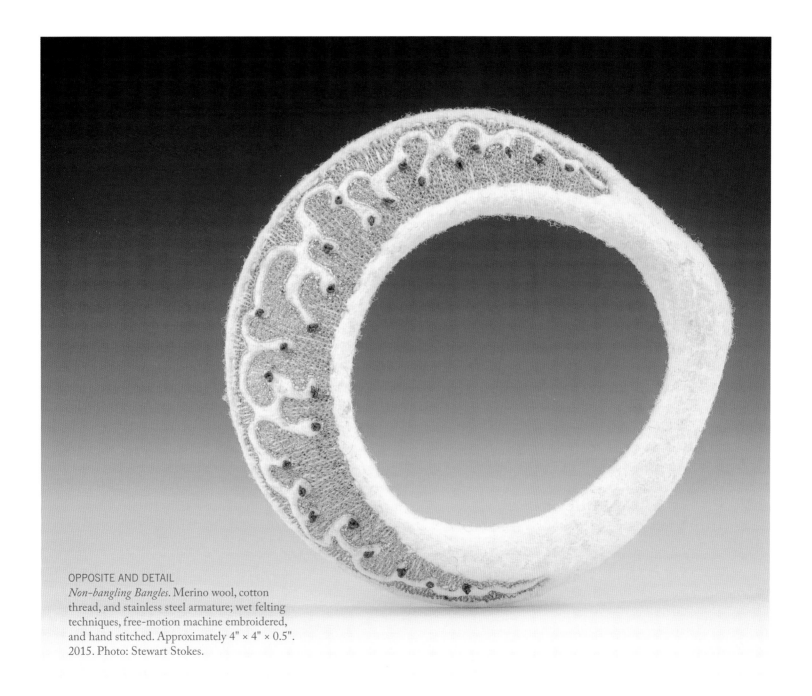

OPPOSITE AND DETAIL
Non-bangling Bangles. Merino wool, cotton
thread, and stainless steel armature; wet felting
techniques, free-motion machine embroidered,
and hand stitched. Approximately 4" × 4" × 0.5".
2015. Photo: Stewart Stokes.

Mariko Kusumoto
Lexington, Massachusetts

I am both fascinated and amused by the ability of synthetic fabric to permanently memorize shapes when heated. Many of my heat-set pieces come from accidental discoveries. During the experimental process, there is sometimes a breathtaking moment; I catch those moments and develop ideas from that point.

I love the translucency of fabric. Using layers and adding moving parts create playful, mysterious, and ethereal atmospheres. Although I am a metalsmith, I was immediately drawn into this fabric world, which is the complete opposite of metal. I feel endless, unlimited possibilities in these materials.

My work has been presented at museums and galleries across the United States, and has been included in the permanent collections of the Swiss National Museum, Switzerland; the Racine Art Museum, Wisconsin; and the Morikami Museum and Japanese Gardens, Delray Beach, Florida.

Organic Sound. Necklace. Polyester. 12" × 12". 2015.
All art images courtesy of Mobilia Gallery.

Blue Bubbles. Detail at upper right. Necklace. Polyester. 16" × 12". 2014.

Germination. Brooch. Polyester. 2" × 2". 2015.

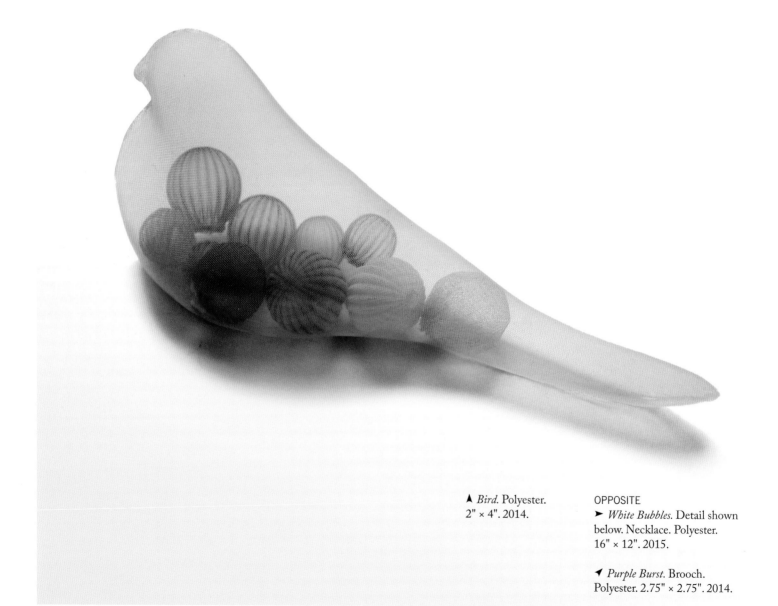

▲ *Bird.* Polyester.
2" × 4". 2014.

OPPOSITE
➤ *White Bubbles.* Detail shown
below. Necklace. Polyester.
16" × 12". 2015.

◄ *Purple Burst.* Brooch.
Polyester. 2.75" × 2.75". 2014.

I create innovative jewelry out of nylon mesh, a material once used as a purely structural element in hats and clothing. The beauty of nylon mesh is that it is, on the one hand, sturdy and structural, but also delicate. It is this juxtaposition that continues to drive my work.

My latest pieces are based on a kind of controlled unraveling. The skeletal forms are constructed using a technique I developed by carefully applying heat to shape and structure the material into new forms, resulting in ethereal, delicate, and otherworldly pieces. It is the tension between solid structure and fragility that continues to interest me as I explore new ways of working with the material.

Michal Lando
Brooklyn, New York

Desert Brooch 1. Brooch. Nylon mesh and sterling silver thread. 4" × 3.5". 2016.

Desert Pendant 1. Necklace/Brooch. Nylon mesh and sterling silver thread. 5.5" × 4.25". 2016.

Divided Landscape. Necklace.
Nylon mesh and sterling silver
thread. 2016.

All art images courtesy of
Dan Sagarin, Mohican Studios.

Landscape in Pink. Necklace. Nylon mesh and
sterling silver thread. 2016.

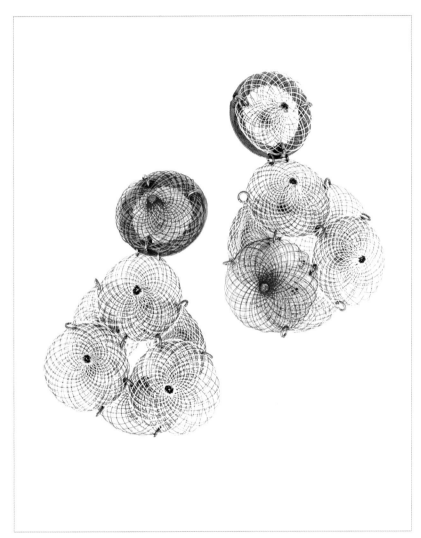

Untitled. Earrings. Nylon mesh and sterling silver. 3" × 2". 2016.

Desert Pendant 2. Necklace/Brooch. Nylon mesh, sterling silver, and steel thread. 6.75" × 3.5". 2016.

Tina Lazzarine
Hammond, Indiana

Sewing has been a creative outlet of mine since childhood. From my mother and my grandmother, I learned cross-stitch, embroidery, and crochet, as well as how to operate a sewing machine. Now, as a metalsmith and fiber artist, I enjoy the challenge of combining textiles with metals in a way that is balanced and gives traditional women's craft a voice in contemporary mixed media sculpture.

My recent work uses the collar to demonstrate the complex identity of woman as both oppressed and empowered. Although feminist activism and social awareness have been instrumental in the advancement of an egalitarian society, a patriarchal mind-set that clouds views on women still persists today. By binding soft fabric with wire into either protruding or constricting forms, sometimes both, my work becomes a metaphor for subjugation. Integral to the work are the dichotomies of hard and soft, seduction and repulsion, protection and intimidation. This complexity parallels the multifaceted aspect of the female experience. The question that remains for the viewer is whether the wearer of the collar is in control—or under it.

Mourning Glory. Kumo shibori cotton, nickel, steel, and glass beads. 20" × 22" × 2". 2012.

OPPOSITE
Something Borrowed. Organza, thread, glass pearls, kumo shibori silk, nickel, velvet, brass, and padlock. 18" × 12" × 12". 2013.

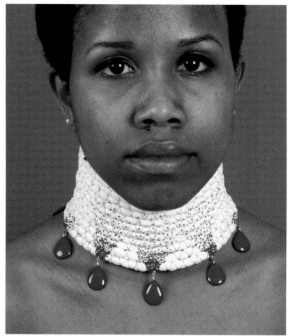

Power Play. Copper, kumo shibori cotton, brass, and leather. 3.5" × 8" × 11.5". 2013.

Heirloom. Kumo shibori cotton, brass, copper, enamel, thread, and lock. 4" × 5" × 5". 2013.

Medusa. Kumo shibori silk, brass, steel, copper, microfiber, silk organza, and thread. 27" × 12" × 18". 2013.

The jewelry I create is inspired by my love for adornment, an interest in patterns and line, and a sense of functionality. Working primarily with steel allows me to build large yet lightweight forms; the addition of fiber gives a contrasting warmth and softness. The bold, pattern-based format of my jewelry has a strong presence when being worn as well as when on display, and the physical movement and variety of textures deliver a rewarding tactile experience in the hand.

I received my BFA in Jewelry and Metalsmithing from Edinboro University of Pennsylvania in 2012. Since graduating, I have worked at such craft institutions as Haystack Mountain School of Craft in Maine, and Peters Valley Craft Center in New Jersey. In 2014-2015, I was selected as a resident artist at the Houston Center for Contemporary Craft.

Jera Rose Petal Lodge
Meadville, Pennsylvania

Wicked. Steel, nickel, mohair, freshwater pearls, and cubic zirconia. 14" × 14" × 3". 2012. Photographer: Hannah Bailey.

Centric Bracelet Trio. Steel and
mohair. 7" × 7" × 2". 2013.

Recherché. Necklace. Powder coated steel, nickel, mohair, freshwater pearls, and cubic zirconia; fabricated and needle-felted. 14" × 14" × 8". 2013. Photographer: Nash Quinn.

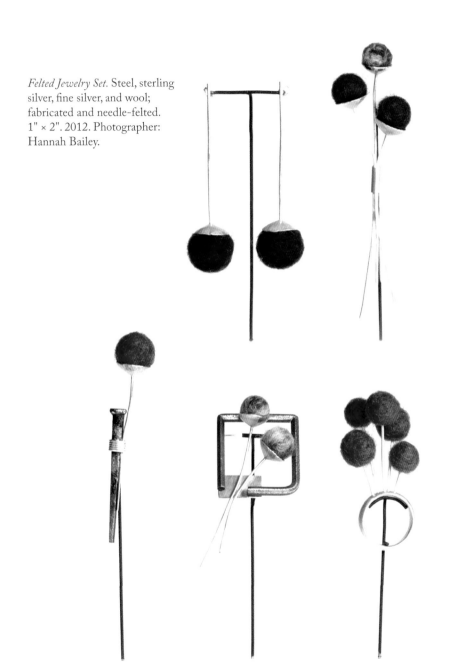

Felted Jewelry Set. Steel, sterling silver, fine silver, and wool; fabricated and needle-felted. 1" × 2". 2012. Photographer: Hannah Bailey.

Cascade. Necklace. Steel and wool; fabricated and needle-felted. 18" × 8" × 2". 2012. Photographer: Hannah Bailey.

Jaclyn Mayer
Brooklyn, New York

Orly Genger by Jaclyn Mayer (OGJM) is a jewelry collaboration between artist Orly Genger and me. Using rope as her main medium, Orly transforms large public spaces, such as Madison Square Park in New York City, into abstract and surreal environments. The jewelry uses the same mediums to construct minimal and organic shapes that are, like the art, both structural and playful. Since the brand's inception in 2009, OGJM has graced the pages of many publications including *Vogue, Elle, Harper's Bazaar,* and *Surface.* We have also done collaborations with brands such as WHIT, Lela Rose, J.Crew, VPL, and most recently, Mara Hoffman.

Baldwin Necklace for WHIT. Hand-painted enamel on climbing rope with casted metal tubes. 12" long. 2012.

All art images courtesy of OGJM Inc.

Asteria Necklace for VPL. Hand-painted enamel on knotted climbing rope. 18" long. 2012.

Reese Bangles. Hand-painted enamel over knitted wire and resin. Various sizes. 2014.

Karma Necklaces for VPL.
Hand-painted enamel on
climbing rope with carved
wood. 25" long. 2013.

Annabelle Bracelets. Hand-painted enamel on climbing rope. 2014.

Cielo Pessione
Amelia, Italy

I am fascinated by the simple tools and techniques of crochet. Its history is tied to women's work, to places in the home with a domestic dimension: the armchair by the window, the sofa in front of the fireplace, or the chair near the doorway. Yet I have also experienced the comfort of places like those between mountainous rocks near breathtaking horizons or on the edge of a seat on a stifling, crowded train. Crochet can emerge from such an intimate setting and carry the meaning of thoughts and actions that go beyond into a different dimension—that of art and its public, shared values.

The time it takes to do this work is precious time, devoted to the pursuit of beauty, its fairness and its logic. Armed with crocheting tools that allow me to be nomadic, I make a daily commitment to time, working against the spread of simple "touch-and-go."

"Pezzi di Cielo" is a line of accessories created as unique, one-of-a-kind pieces or produced in extremely small series. My philosophy is to recycle, and each wearable piece, whether a necklace, hat, or bag, is for me a small sculpture.

Cleo Collar. Metallic, viscose, silk, and nylon. 2012.

164

Carousel Collar. Wool and silk. 2006.

Duet Collar. Wool, silk, carnelian stone, pearl, straw. 2015.

Green Collar. Cotton and mother of pearl. 2015.

Crazy Red Collar. Cotton, glass, and hematite. 2014.

I delight in the magical surrealism of reality in nature. My designs are informed by my studies of entomology and life sciences, as well as my experiences living in the tropics and in the desert. I savor researching and revisiting the realm of anomalous plants and animals. With this comes the humble reminder that we are just one species in a multitude of interdependent creatures. We are defined as human beings by our need to create personal adornment and art; thus, I feel a connection to a continuum of artisans.

As a fiber artist now working with metal, I find that after thirty-plus years, I am still striving to turn straw into gold. Textile patterns and textures fixed into metal evoke memories of the traditional textiles and basketry I encountered while living abroad. Translating fiber techniques into silver, gold, and other metals continues to fascinate me. With a weaver's eye for color, I explore the processes of applying patinas and enamels in my work.

Jeanie Pratt
Nipomo, California

Una Ala #1. Brooch. Copper, niobium, sterling silver, opal; looped, anodized, etched, and fabricated. 2.5" × 2". 2007. Photo: Carol Holaday.

OPPOSITE
Mariposa. Necklace. Argentium silver, fine silver, 24K gold, 22K gold, 18K gold, niobium, copper, abalone, fossilized coral, labradorite, rutilated quartz, quartz crystal, opals, carnelian, freshwater cultured pearls, glass, enamel, blue mountain swallowtail wing, Eastern Tiger Swallowtail wing; Cloisonné enamel, hand woven and enameled copper and gold, looped gold inlaid in enamel, Viking knit, lashed, anodized, etched, fabricated. 18" necklace with 2.375" counterbalance. 2015. Photo: Hap Sakwa.

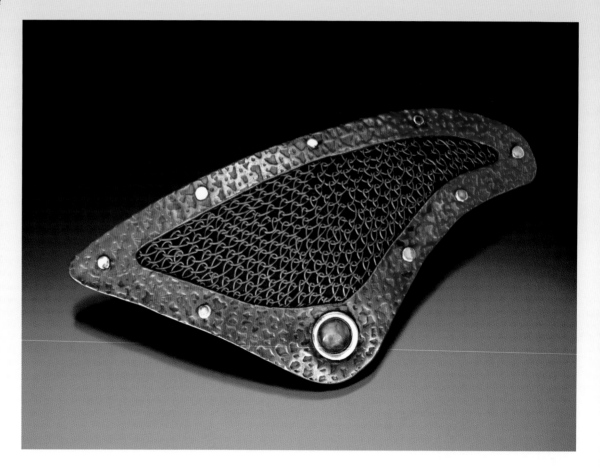

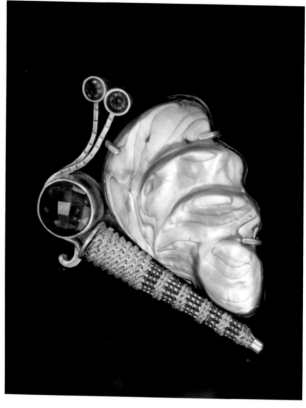

Exotic Origins. Necklace. Sterling (Argentium) silver, fine silver, niobium, bronze, copper, gold/Argentium silver, bubble azurite, fire agate, amber with insect inclusions, opal, Mexican opal, topaz, star rutilated quartz, citrine, chalcedony, sunstone, glass cabochon, freshwater pearl, butterfly wings, beetle wings, enamel; hand knit, hand woven, bobbin lace, looped, lashed, enameled, embossed, etched, fabricated, anodized, and oxidized. 18" necklace with 3" counterbalance. 2012. Photo: Steve Rossman.

Mariposa del Mar. Brooch. Sterling silver, fine silver, copper, smoky quartz, green topaz; hand woven (twined and Soumak), etched, fabricated. 1.75" × 1.5". 2011. Photo: Carol Holaday.

OPPOSITE
Flight of Fancy. Necklace. Sterling silver, fine silver, niobium, gold, tourmaline, druzy, opal, ammolite, abalone, freshwater pearl, insect wings, enamel, resin; hand knit, bobbin lace, enameled, lashed, etched, fabricated, anodized, and oxidized. 18". 2011. Photo: Hap Sakwa.

Cara Romano
Bar Harbor, Maine

Over the past decade, I have taken cues from color, geometry, and textiles to create contemporary work that maintains a connection to the past through techniques and craftsmanship. I dip merino wool roving in hot soap and water, then agitate the fibers in a circular motion in my hands, resulting in a solid mass of felted wool that is both durable and vibrant. I can then set the felt piece like a stone or use it as a bead in my metal work. By employing simple forms such as squares and circles, I allow the viewer to focus on my textile manipulation.

Some of the more recent accolades of my work include an award of excellence from the American Craft Council in 2010; participation in *From Minimal to Bling: Contemporary Studio Jewelry* at the Society of Arts and Crafts, Boston in 2013; an Artist Project Grant from the Maine Arts Commission in 2015; and serving as President of the Maine Crafts Association from 2010 to 2016.

Abacus Brooch. Sterling silver and merino wool; agitation felting. 2.75" × 2.75" × 0.25". 2005. Photo by Robert Diamante.

Riveted Felt Necklace. Sterling silver and merino wool; agitation
felting. 18" × 5" × 0.25". 2010. Photo by Hap Sakawa.

▲ *Pivot Felted Silver Three Drop Earrings.*
Sterling silver and merino wool; agitation felting.
3.50" × 0.25" × 0.25". 2013. Photo by Ralph Gabriner.

► *Pivot Felted Silver Fringe Necklace.* Sterling silver
and merino wool; agitation felting. 18" × 4" × 0.25".
2013. Photo by Ralph Gabriner.

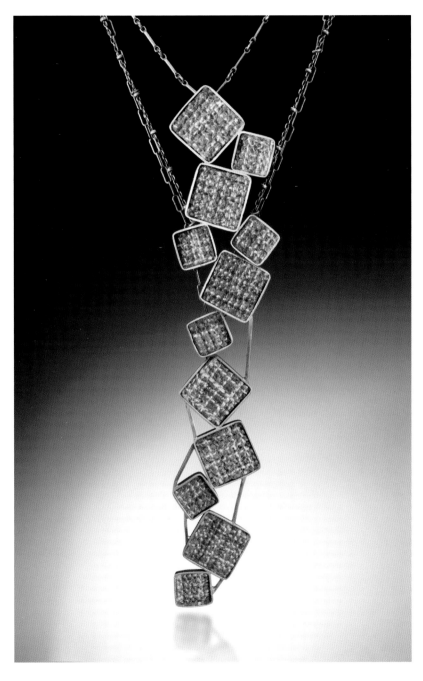

◄ *Cascading Stitched Felt Necklace*. Silver, merino wool, and cotton; needle felted. 38" × 3" × 0.25". 2014. Photo by Ralph Gabriner.

▼ *Stitched Felt meets Felted Silver*. Sterling silver, merino wool, and cotton; agitation felting. 4" × 0.25" × 0.25". 2014. Photo by Ralph Gabriner.

Elena Rosenberg
Scarsdale, New York

In my textile jewelry, I want to capture the exquisite gracefulness and irresistible expressiveness of botanical forms. I don't draw from the standard crochet stitch arsenal; instead, I maneuver the hook and silk yarn free-form, creating unconventional, unrecognizable stitch combinations. Some of my stalks, stems, petals, and leaves have identifiable, lifelike features; others are contrived, fantastical specimens. I forage for inspiration in botanical gardens, plant nurseries, on the shore at low tide—wherever plants are found. My necklaces, lariats, pendants, bracelets, and rings are unabashedly whimsical and playful. They are conversation starters, they are morsels of haptic delight.

There is a tradition of working with textiles among the women in my family: one of my grandmothers was masterful with the sewing machine, and the other grandmother did traditional handweaving. As a child, I learned to knit and crochet from my mother and rediscovered knitting in my late twenties. I have been designing, creating limited edition collections, exhibiting my work, and publishing my knitting patterns since 2007. I have shown my hand-knit and crochet fashion at the

Philadelphia Museum of Art Craft Show, the American Craft Council Show, CraftBoston, and other juried exhibitions of fine craft, and I am the recipient of the 2014 NICHE Award in Fashion Accessories. I am active in art and craft advocacy, and serve on the board of directors for both the Surface Design Association and the Pennsylvania Guild of Craftsmen.

OPPOSITE

◄ *Terra Cotta Collier Necklace, Cuff Bracelet, and Ring.* Mulberry silk; free-form crochet. 2014. Courtesy of Ellen Crane.

▼ *Botanical Lace Bracelet.* Mulberry silk; free-form crochet. 2013.

▲ *Sea Kelp Necklace II.*
Mulberry silk. 2013.

► *Sea Kelp Necklace.* Mulberry
silk; free-form crochet. 2013.

Land and Sea Bracelets. Merino wool, silk, cotton; wet felting. 2016.

My needlework necklaces express my love of diverse cultures and their imagery. The central theme of my work is human consciousness, which I envision as fragments of the mind. These colorful and intimate portraits portray layered emotional states, such as self-identity and issues of morality, sexuality, and memory. These are all common global conditions, natural to everyone who shares our planet.

With a varied grounding in art, theater costume design, graphic design, and floral artistry, I have discovered that I enjoy working on a diminutive and very detailed scale, both on and off the body. In addition to my necklaces, I create couture-level tambour work compositions.

As an educator, I have taught fiber classes to both children and adults and find these activities a stimulating adjunct to my own art practice. I have recently been instrumental in founding the San Diego Textile Study Guild, a non-profit organization of both beginning and established fiber artists. Reaching across textile methods and styles, we are interested in learning about all aspects of the field. By sharing this knowledge, we hope to foster creativity and encourage an expanded view of this vibrant field.

Caroline Rousset-Johnson
San Diego, California

Shore. Necklace. Cotton threads, sea beads, metal, and plastic ring. 11" × 11". 2015.

All art images courtesy of Adriana Zuniga-Williams.

Link (detail). Necklace. Cotton threads, sea beads, metal, and plastic ring. 11.5" × 14". 2014.

Comet. Necklace. Cotton threads, sea beads, metal, and plastic ring. 11.5" × 15". 2014.

Dolmas. Necklace. Cotton threads, sea beads, metal, and plastic ring. 10" × 13.5". 2014.

Photo by Maria Rudavská.

Zuzana Graus Rudavská
Bratislava, Slovakia

I was born in Bratislava into a family of professional artists. Influenced by their artwork and by watching them work, I naturally became an artist. I studied fiber art at the College of Fine Arts and Crafts and at the Academy of Arts and Architecture in Prague and over the years, experimented with fiber or fiber techniques in various media and materials both in Europe and the United States.

In my work, I am inspired by the quality and essence of my materials; in many instances, a piece can have solid or translucent expression depending on the light. As I approach each piece, I explore the possibilities of creating contrast between solid and transparent, smooth and textured, rigid and flexible. The combination of strict basic geometric forms with textured, woven, or interlaced fragments inside of them allows me to achieve even greater compositional contrast. For me, designing jewelry is like creating a small sculpture, something to hold in the hand and touch. My greatest inspiration is nature, where different materials of various qualities coexist. I create my jewelry in the hope that in this age of technology my piece will reconnect the wearer with nature itself, my greatest inspiration of all.

Citrine Brooch III. Sterling silver, gold-filled wire, and citrine. 2.67" × 2.67" × 0.11". 2004. Photo: Milan Maťašovský.

OPPOSITE
Wire shawl. Sterling silver and polished hematite stone. 45" × 12.6" × 0.4". 2010. Photo: Oto Skalicky.

Green Crystal Brooches. Sterling silver, gold-filled wire, peridot, and labradorite. Approximate size: 2.67" × 2.67" × 0.11" each. 2006. Photo: Oto Skalicky.

▲ *Pearl Brooch*. Sterling silver, gold-filled wire, peridot, and labradorite. Approximate size: 2.55" × 3.42" × 0.31". 2002. Photo: Milan Maťašovský.

◀ *Geometric Pearl Brooch*. Sterling silver, gold-filled wire, freshwater natural and dyed pearls. 2.91" × 2.91" × 0.23". 2004. Photo: Milan Maťašovský.

▶ *Two Crystal Bracelets*. Sterling silver, gold-filled wire, citrine, carneol/fluorite, and labradorite. 2.67" × 2.67" × 0.11" each. 2004. Photo: Milan Maťašovský.

Courtesy of Tiffany Whitfield.

Kathryn Scimone Stanko
Pittsburgh, Pennsylvania

I named my art MetaLace®, a metamorphosis of unorganized, twisted metal created into works of order, shape, beauty, and purpose. As an educator, curator, and artist, my inspiration for jewelry and sculptural adornment originated from travel in and study of East Asia and Africa. My designs are influenced and informed by the woven basketry of African women's co-op groups and the beauty of African gemstones; the seasonal woodblock prints of Hiroshige and Hokusai; and the stunning jades and pearls of East Asia. I create these non-traditional works of sterling, copper, and gold wearable art using traditional fiber techniques, at times accented with semi-precious stones, pearls, handcrafted glass, or re-purposed fibers.

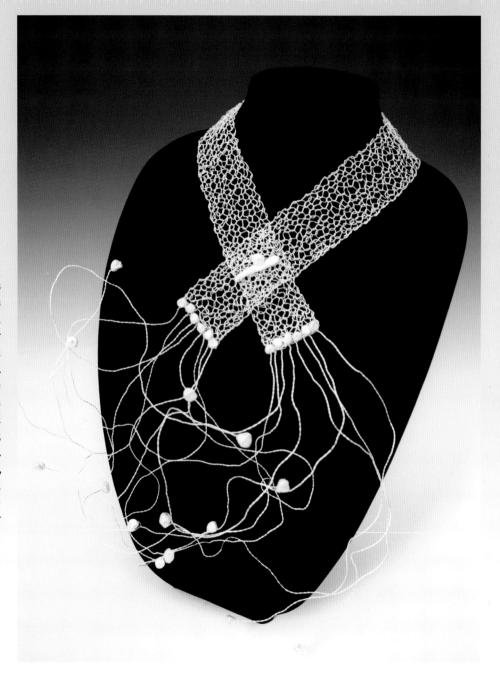

A Single Strand of Sterling. Sterling silver wire and freshwater pearls. 18" × 12". 2013. Courtesy of Tiffany Whitfield.

Leaves of Sterling with Pearl Berries. Oxidized sterling silver wire and freshwater pearls. 8" × 9". 2015. Courtesy of Tiffany Whitfield.

Floral Burst of Copper. Copper wire and recycled Kenyan glass beads. 12" × 9". 2014. Courtesy of Tiffany Whitfield.

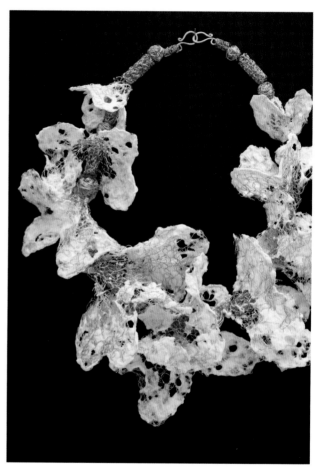

Works on Paper I. Copper wire and cotton linter pulp. 18" × 16". 2014. Courtesy of Tiffany Whitfield.

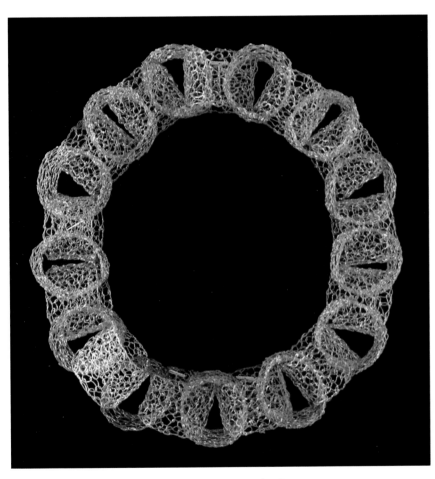

Adornment in Mixed Metals. Copper, sterling, and oxidized sterling wire. 11" × 11". 2010.

Mannequin in MetaLace®. Treated copper wire and repurposed mannequin. 57" × 16". 2012. Courtesy of Tiffany Whitfield.

It is always intriguing to see how my personal imagination and inspiration are embodied in an actual object. The working process is more open towards momentary happenings rather than manipulated by preset intention, which brings unexpected value. Rather, I explore, experience, and cultivate the moment.

I often observe how different elements play out in their own way, helping to define the destiny of each work. Pursuing the textures of abundant materials is my primal interest in jewelry. Adopting different fibers with other solid material reveals unique surfaces, characteristics, shapes, colors, and textures from which arise emotion, balance, and tension. This is the most fascinating part of my work.

Myung Urso
Rochester, New York

Blue Touch. Brooch. Cotton, silk, ink, thread, sterling silver, and lacquer; sewing, calligraphy, and soldering. 4" × 4.5" × 1". 2016.

Combination. Necklace. Silk, silicone bands, Hanji (Korean paper), Asian ink, sterling silver, and lacquer; sewing, calligraphy, and soldering. 8.25" × 9.5" × 1.5". 2014.

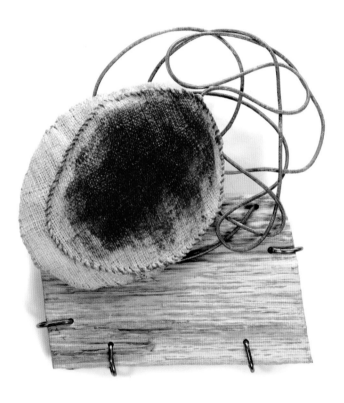

Moonlight. Brooch. Ramie, wood, sterling silver, steel wire, and pigment; sewing and soldering. 4" × 4" × 0.75". 2015.

Cloud. Brooch. Silk organza, thread, wood, acrylic paint, and sterling silver; sewing and soldering. 5.75" × 4" × 1". 2015.

Morphe. Necklace. Cotton, thread, sterling silver, and
lacquer; sewing and soldering. 10.5" × 10.5" × 1". 2015.

Lisa Van Herik
La Jolla, California

I started my artistic career hand painting jewelry; over the years, I studied metalsmithing, surface design, glass art, abstract art, and interior design. I was, and still am, fascinated by materials of all kinds and especially entranced by making something beautiful from something ordinary, combining incongruous elements into something wholly new and unexpected. It is that challenge that propels me to make art while always trying to make it unique and exciting. Experimentation is at the heart of my work.

When learning metalsmithing, I became taken with wire weaving and all its possibilities. Often driven by color and texture, my work with wire expanded to include colored wires and fiber. The success of my first book, *Make Wire Beads*, led to *Fiber Wire Beads and Jewelry*, where I created the "wiber"—a joined strand of both fiber and wire as a new art element. Visual warmth meets constructive strength. As I continue to explore various wire weaving techniques, I have created some of my own original techniques seen here. The movement of the line, the search to see how far I can push and morph the wire, is a constant, delicious pursuit.

Expanse. Neck pendant. Simple weave in fine and sterling silvers. 2015.

All images courtesy of Mark Goros.

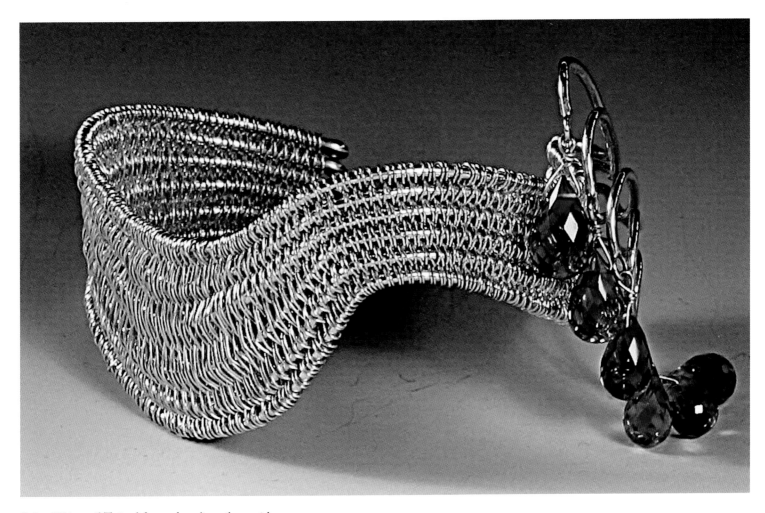

Reign. Wrist cuff. Twined fine and sterling silvers with
faceted amethyst briolettes. 2009.

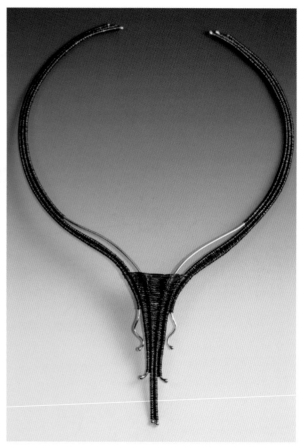

Victoria. Necklace. Coil woven bronze wires. 2007.

Grace. Neckpiece. Twined sterling and
enamel copper coated wires. 2011.

Intricacy. Braided bracelets. Stained aluminum wire and sterling. 2014.

Sayumi Yokouchi
Brooklyn, New York

In my work, I employ strategies of repetition and systems of order using various materials. I am interested in the point when materials and processes become the site for making work. I sometimes revisit the old site to find a new site. It all begins with wonderful randomness of thought and imagination that are formed by the collection of inspirations and questions around the materials themselves, which I visually translate into my language.

My cultural background (Japanese) has inspired me greatly. Being born and raised in the city of Tokyo cultivated my curiosity for the natural world. Nature has quietly yet forcefully coexisted in modern-day Japanese life; I found man-made nature and representation of natural objects to be more natural. It is probably without my conscious intent that this unique balance between real and artificial shaped my fascination and led me to design something tangible and unusual in small, wearable objects.

The clustered and bundled elements I create over the surface of my jewelry are, to me, much like the life of lichens. They are unique creatures of intricate ornamentation and intimate patterns of organisms, which seem to resemble the community we humans inhabit.

GARDENS—frost. Brooch. Polishing felt buffs, dye, paint, thread, silver 925, and palladium. 2.75" × 2.75" × 1.57". 2015.

GARDENS—secret. Brooch. Polishing felt buffs, bone, coffee, tea, abrasive stones, thread, silver 925, and palladium. 3.15" × 3.15" × 1.57". 2014.

GARDENS—snow. Brooch. Polishing felt buffs, coral, dye, tea, thread, silver 925, and palladium. 3.54" × 3.15" × 1.57". 2014.

COPIA. Brooch. Polishing felt buffs, dye, thread, silver 925, and white gold. 2.75" × 2.75" × 1.96". 2006.

GARDENS—passage.
Brooch. Polishing felt buffs,
bone, coffee, tea, thread,
silver 925, and palladium.
3.54" × 3.54" × 1.18". 2014.

ARTISTS' WEBSITES AND CONTACT INFORMATION

Luis Acosta
www.luisacosta.nl

Susan Taber Avila
www.suta.com

Anastasia Azure
www.anastasiaazure.com

Laura G. Berman
www.lauragberman.com

Eva Camacho-Sánchez
www.lanahandmade.com

Lauri Chambers
www.laurichambers.com

David K. Chatt
www.davidchatt.com

Susan Kathleen Doyle
www.susankathleendoyle.com

Evy Edelman
www.designsbyevy.com

Arline M. Fisch
afisch@mail.sdsu.edu

Jenne Giles
www.harlequinfeltworks.com

Ania Gilmore
www.aniaart.com

Ana Lisa Hedstrom
www.analisahedstrom.com

Daiga Henson and
Sarmite Svilis
www.sarmite.com

Jean Hicks
www.jeanhicks.com

Maja Houtman
www.majahoutman.nl

Carol and Jean-Pierre Hsu
www.hsustudios.com

Małgosia Kalińska
www.malgosiakalinska.com

Sharon Kallis
www.sharonkallis.com

Yong Joo Kim
www.yongjookim.com

Lisa Klakulak
www.strongfelt.com

Mariko Kusumoto
www.marikokusumoto.com

Michal Lando
www.michallandodesign.com

Tina Lazzarine
www.tinalazzarine.com

Jera Rose Petal Lodge
www.jeralodge.com

Ariane Mariane
www.arianemariane.com

Jaclyn Mayer (Orly Genger)
www.jaclynmayer.com

Amy Nguyen
www.amynguyentextiles.com

Matilda Norberg
www.matildanorberg.se

Cielo Pessione
www.cielopessione.it

Jeanie Pratt
www.jeaniepratt.net

Claire Prebble
www.claireprebble.com

Della Reams
www.dellareams.com

Leisa Rich
www.monaleisa.com

K. Riley
www.krileywearableart.
squarespace.com

Cara Romano
www.cararomano.com

Elena Rosenberg
www.elenarosenberg.com

Caroline Rousset-Johnson
www.about.me/
carolineroussetjohnson

Zuzana Graus Rudavská
www.zuzanagrausrudavska.com

Carole Simcox
cmakeup@shaw.ca

Kathryn Scimone Stanko
www.metalace.net

Myung Urso
www.myungurso.com

Lisa Van Herik
www.studiovanherik.com

Anne Vincent
www.annevincent.com

Rebecca Wendlandt
www.rebeccawendlandt.com

Sayumi Yokouchi
www.sayumiyokouchi.com

Laverne Zabielski
www.LaverneZ.com

GALLERIES AND EXHIBITION SPACES

Artists featured in this book have exhibited at the following galleries and exhibition spaces.

NEW ENGLAND

Alchemy 9.2.5
Belmont, MA 02478
www.alchemy925.com

browngrotta arts
Wilton, CT 06897
www.browngrotta.com

Dow Studio
Deer Isle, ME 04627
www.dowstudiodeerisle.com

Fire Opal
Brookline, MA 02446
www.fire-opal.com

(KoT) Contemporary Craft
Ellsworth, ME 04605
www.kotcontemporarycraft.com

Lacoste Gallery
Concord, MA 01742
www.lacostegallery.com

Lana Handmade
Easthampton, MA 01027
www.lanahandmade.com

Mobilia Gallery
Cambridge, MA 02138
www.mobilia-gallery.com

The Society of Arts and Crafts
Boston, MA 02210
www.societyofcrafts.org

The Worcester Center for Crafts
Worcester, MA 01605
www.worcestercraftcenter.org

THE MID-ATLANTIC

American Art Marketing
New York, NY 10019
www.anamericancraftsman.com

Ann Ahn
New York, NY 10021
www.ptaylorclothing.com/location/
ann-ahn/

Chocolate Moose
Washington, DC 20036
www.chocolatemoosedc.com

The Eclectic Collector
Katonah, NY 10536
www.theeclecticcollector.com

The Fallingwater Museum
Mill Run, PA 15464
www.fallingwatermuseumstore.org

Heidi Lowe Gallery
Rehoboth Beach, DE 19971
www.heidilowejewelry.com

Jewelers Werk Gallery
Washington, DC 20007
www.jewelerswerk.com

Phipps Conservatory and
Botanical Gardens Store
Pittsburgh, PA 15213
www.phipps.conservatory.org

Pittsburgh Center for the Arts
Pittsburgh, PA 15232
www.center.pfpca.org

The Store LTD
Baltimore, MD 21210

WAX
Pittsburgh, PA 15232
www.waxjewelrydesignstudio.com

Woodmere Art Museum
Gift Shop
Philadelphia, PA 19118
www.woodmereartmuseum.org

Zenith Gallery
Washington, DC 20012
www.zenithgallery.com

THE SOUTH

A Mixed Bag
Pinellas Park, FL 33782

Appalachian Fireside Gallery
Berea, KY 40403
www.visitberea.com/appalachian-
fireside-gallery

Arrowmont School of
Arts and Crafts
Gatlinburg, TN 37738
www.arrowmont.org

Bella Arte Gallery
Midlothian, VA 23113
www.bellaarte.com

Bellagio Art to Wear
Asheville, NC 28803
www.bellagioarttowear.com

The Byrne Gallery
Middleburg, VA 20117
www.byrnegallery.com

Carlyn Galerie
Dallas, TX 75225
www.carlyngalerie.com

Crescent Moon
Wilmington, NC 28401
www.crescentmoonnc.com

Dream Weaver Collection
Sarasota, FL 34236
www.dreamweavercollection.com

Great Artists Collective
New Orleans, LA 70116
www.greatartistscollective.com

Hands On Gallery
Key West, FL 33040
www.handsongallery.com

Houston Center for
Contemporary Craft
Houston, TX 77002
www.crafthouston.org

Ice House Artists' Co-op
Berkeley Springs, WV 25411
www.icehousecoop.com

Kentucky Artisan Center
Berea, KY 40403
www.kentuckyartisancenter.ky.gov

Koi Gallery
Louisville, KY 40299
www.looklouisvilleart.com/members
/koi-gallery

Light Art + Design
Chapel Hill, NC 27516
www.lightartdesign.com

The Little Gallery on Smith Mountain
Lake
Moneta, VA 24121
www.thelittlegallerysml.com

Mora Contemporary Jewelry
Asheville, NC 28801
www.moracollection.com

Mountain Laurel Gallery
Berkeley Springs, WV 25411
www.mountainlaurelgallery.com

M.S. Rezny Gallery
Lexington, KY 28801
www.msrezny.com

Penland Gallery
Penland, NC 28705
www.penland.org

Studio 40
Lewisburg, WV 24901
www.janska.com/studio-40,-inc-

Wear Art Thou
Austin, TX 78756
www.wearartthouaustin.com

THE MIDWEST

Flux Metal Arts Gallery
Mentor, OH 44060
www.fluxmetalarts.com

Good Goods
Saugatuck, MI 49453
www.goodgoods.com

John Michael Kohler
Arts Center
Sheboygan, WI 53081
www.jmkac.org

Leedy-Voulkos Gallery
Kansas City, MO 64108
www.leedy-voulkos.com

Pistachios
Chicago, IL 60611
www.pistachiosonline.com

Poppy
Columbia, MO 65201
www.poppymadebyhand.com

Tallulah Belle's
Leawood, KS 66211
www.tallulahbelles.com

UMMA Store | University of Michigan
Museum of Art
Ann Arbor, MI 48109
www.umma.umich.edu/visiting/shop.html

Wantoot Gallery
Mineral Point, WI 53565
www.wantoot.com

THE WEST

J. Cotter Gallery
Vail, CO 81658
www.jcottergallery.com

Outnumbered Gallery
Littleton, CO 80120
www.outnumberedgallery.com

Patina Gallery
Santa Fe, NM 87501
www.patina-gallery.com

Piece Art Gallery
Vail, CO 81657
www.pieceartgallery.com

Santa Fe Weaving Gallery
Santa Fe, NM 87501
www.sfweaving.com

Tresa Vorenberg Goldsmiths
Santa Fe, NM 87501
www.Tvgoldsmiths.com

Woodbury Jewelers
Park City, UT 84060
www.woodburyjewelers.com

THE PACIFIC WEST

The Alexander Gallery
Nevada City, CA 95959
www.thealexandergallery.net

de Young Museum Store
San Francisco, CA 94118
www.famsf.org

Earth Spirits
Palm Desert, CA 92260
www.earthspiritspalmdesert.com

Earthworks Galleries
Yachats, OR 97498
www.earthworksgalleries.net

Fine Eye Gallery
Sutter Creek, CA 95685
www.fineeye.com

Hallie Ford Museum of Art,
Willamette University
Salem, Oregon 97301
www.willamette.edu/arts/hfma

HumanArts
Ojai, CA 93023
www.humanartsgallery.com

Imagine
Santa Barbara, CA 93108

Mingei Museum Shop
San Diego, CA 92101
www.mingei.org

Pomegranate
La Jolla, CA 92037
www.pomegranatelajolla.com

The Rafael's
San Francisco, CA 94104
www.therafaels.com

Studio Seven Arts
Pleasanton, CA 94566
www.studiosevenarts.com

Taboo Studio
San Diego, CA 92103
www.taboostudio.net

Velvet da Vinci Gallery
San Francisco, CA 94109
www.velvetdavinci.com

The Websters
Ashland, OR 97520
www.yarnatwebsters.com

INTERNATIONAL

Galeria Sztuki w Legnicy
Legnica, Poland
www.galeria.legnica.pl

Galeria YES
Poznan, Poland
www.galeriayes.pl

Galerie Beeld & Aambeeld
Enschede, The Netherlands
www.beeldenaambeeld.nl

Galerie Bijzonder-Heden
Zwolle, The Netherlands
www.bijzonder-heden.nl

Galerie Wies Willemsen
Amsterdam, The Netherlands
www.wieswillemsen.nl

Galleri Montan
Copenhagen, Denmark
www.montan.dk

Gallery Nori
Jeju Island, South Korea
www.facebook.com/GalleryNori

La Basilica Galeria
Barcelona, Spain
www.labasilicagaleria.com

Thomas Cohn Gallery
São Paulo, Brazil
www.galeriathomascohn.com.br

ZeeZandZilver
The Hague, The Netherlands
www.zeezandzilver.nl

ONLINE

Artful Home
www.artfulhome.com

Klimt.02- Online Art Platform
www.klimt02.net

MUSEUMS

Artists featured in this book have exhibited at or are in the following permanent collections.

American Textile History Museum
Lowell, MA 01854
www.athm.org

Bloomington Center for the Arts
Bloomington, MN 55431
www.bloomingtonmn.gov/facility/
bloomington-center-arts

Cooper Hewitt Museum
New York, NY 10128
www.cooperhewitt.org

Corning Museum of Glass
Corning, NY 14830
www.cmog.org

Dane G. Hansen
Memorial Museum
Logan, KS 67646
www.hansenmuseum.org

de Young | Fine Arts Museums
of San Francisco
San Francisco, CA 94118
www.deyoung.famsf.org

Esse Purse Museum
Little Rock, AR 72202
www.essepursemuseum.com

Fresno Art Museum
Fresno, CA 93703
www.fresnoartmuseum.org

Fuller Craft Museum
Brockton, MA 02301
www.fullercraft.org

The Getty Museum
Los Angeles, CA 90049
www.getty.edu

The Goldstein Museum of Design
University of Minnesota
St. Paul, MN 55108
www.goldstein.design.umn.edu

Solomon R. Guggenheim Museum
New York, NY 10128
www.guggenheim.org

Hirshhorn Museum
Washington, DC 20013
www.hirshhorn.si.edu

Houston Center for
Contemporary Craft
Houston, TX 77002
www.crafthouston.org

Institute of Contemporary Art
Boston, MA 02210
www.icaboston.org

Kamm Teapot Foundation
Sparta, NC 28675
www.kammteapotfoundation.org

Kentucky Museum of Art
and Craft
Louisville, KY 40202
www.kmacmuseum.org

John Michael Kohler Arts Center
Sheboygan, WI 53081
www.jmkac.org

Madison Museum of
Contemporary Art
Madison, WI 53703
www.mmoca.org

Morikami Museum and
Japanese Gardens
Delray Beach, FL 33446
www.morikami.org

Museum of Arts and Design
New York, NY 10019
www.madmuseum.org

Museum of Craft and Design
San Francisco, CA 94107
www.sfmcd.org

The Craft and Folk Art Museum
Los Angeles, CA 94103
www.cafam.org

Museum of Fine Arts, Boston
Boston, MA 02114
www.mfa.org

New Bedford Art Museum
New Bedford, MA 02740
www.newbedfordart.org

Oakland Museum of California
Oakland, CA 94607
www.museumca.org

Palos Verdes Art Center
Rancho Palos Verdes, CA 90275
www.pvartcenter.org

The Phillips Collection
Washington, DC 20009
www.phillipscollection.org

Racine Art Museum
Racine, WI 53403
www.ramart.org

Renwick Gallery of the
Smithsonian American Art Museum
Washington, DC 20006
www.renwick.americanart.si.edu

Society of Arts and Crafts
Boston, MA 02210
www.societyofcrafts.org

The Tacoma Art Museum
Tacoma, WA 98402
www.tacomaartmuseum.org

The George Washington University
Museum and the Textile Museum
Washington, DC 20052
www.museum.gwu.edu

Yeiser Art Center Gallery
Paducah, KY 42001
www.paducah.travel/listings/yeiser
-art-center/962/

INTERNATIONAL

Atelier De Zilverling
Leiden, The Netherlands
www.atelierdezilverling.com

China National Silk Museum
Hangzhou, China
www.en.chinasilkmuseum.com

Cisternerne – Museum of
Modern Glass Art
Copenhagen, Denmark
www.cisternerne.dk/en

CODA Museum
Apeldoorn, The Netherlands
www.coda-apeldoorn.nl/museum

Finnish Glass Museum
Riihimäki, Finland
www.suomenlasimuseo.fi/

Hangaram Art Museum
Seoul, South Korea
www.sac.or.kr/eng/Space/space_art.jsp

Swiss National Museum
Zürich, Switzerland
www.nationalmuseum.ch/e

SUSAN TABER AVILA

Susan Taber Avila is a professor of design at the University of California, Davis, where she teaches courses in textile design and history of fashion. She is a practicing artist and has exhibited work in Argentina, Canada, China, Costa Rica, Finland, Hong Kong, Lithuania, Mexico, Spain, Swaziland, Turkey, and the United Kingdom, as well as in numerous exhibitions in the United States. Her artwork is included in several books and periodicals, and she has published in *Fiberarts, Ornament, Surface Design Journal,* and *TextilForum.* Examples of her work can be seen at www.suta.com.

MARGERY GOLDBERG

Margery Goldberg began sculpting at a young age while growing up in Rochester, New York, which was a hotbed for woodworking. At George Washington University, wood became her artistic medium, a medium that she uses to sculpt and make art furniture to this day. She opened Zenith Gallery in Washington, DC, in 1978, and in 2000 founded the Zenith Community Arts Foundation, a non-profit dedicated to fostering alliances between artists, businesses, and other organizations in order to use art to benefit the metropolitan community. In Washington, DC, Goldberg has been a member of the Arts Commission, a board member of the Jewish National Museum, and a member of the Downtown Arts Development Task Force. She received the Mayor's Excellence in Service to the Arts award in 2010 for her contribution to the cultural life in the nation's capital.

ANNE LEE
E. ASHLEY ROONEY

As coauthors, Anne Lee and E. Ashley Rooney balance each other and offer different experiences and perspectives: Rooney is the author of over fifty books, specializing in contemporary art and architecture; and Lee has researched, curated, and written about exhibitions at Vose Galleries in Boston. Exploring fiber art together has been a fascinating and fruitful journey they are eager to share. They have also coedited *Encaustic Art in the Twenty-First Century* (Schiffer).